HAUNTED
FLORIDA
ROADSIDE
ATTRACTIONS

HEATHER LEIGH, PhD

Haunted America

Published by Haunted America
A Division of The History Press
Charleston, SC
www.historypress.com

Front cover: A giant dinosaur overlooks I-4 near the entrance to Dinosaur World. *Heather Leigh, PhD*.

First published 2024

Manufactured in the United States

ISBN 9781467156929

Library of Congress Control Number: 2024936751

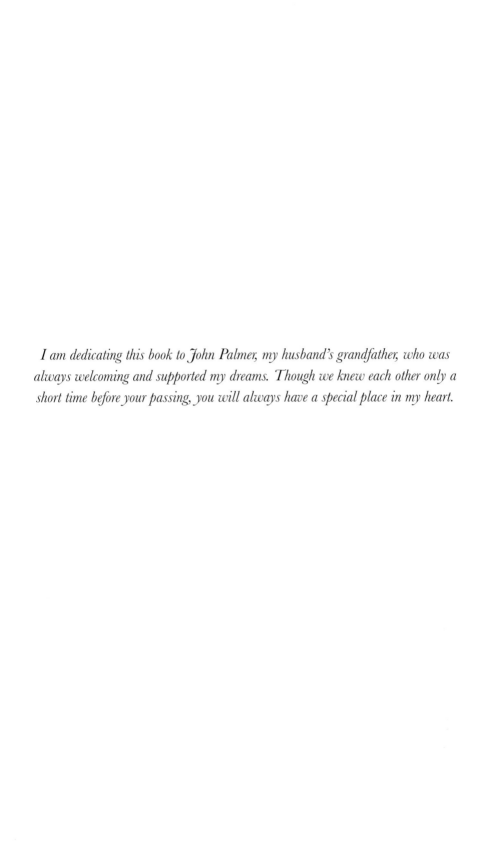

I am dedicating this book to John Palmer, my husband's grandfather, who was always welcoming and supported my dreams. Though we knew each other only a short time before your passing, you will always have a special place in my heart.

CONTENTS

FOREWORD

Few know the shadowed corners of the unknown like my friend Heather Leigh, PhD. With a passion for discovering the truth that rivals any explorer, she has always ventured into the recesses of human experience, unafraid of what might be creeping in the shadows. In this book, she invites you to join her on one journey through the winding alleys of hauntings, where whispers brush against your ear and floorboards creak with spine-tingling stories.

But be warned: this is not just a collection of campfire tales spun for cheap thrills. Heather Leigh writes with a scientist's scrutinizing gaze and a poet's soulful touch. She dissects the anatomy of a haunting, peeling back layers of folklore and psychology to reveal the raw lure at its core.

As you delve into these pages, you'll meet the restless spirits that cling to the fringes of our world, each with their tragic symphony to play. You'll feel the chill of an ancestral phantom. But Heather Leigh reminds us that even the most chilling wraith was once a beating heart, a soul lost in the echoes of time.

What makes this book truly remarkable, however, is its subject matter and the integrity with which it's written. Heather Leigh is no sensationalist. She presents her findings with the meticulous research of a true detective and the open mind of a truth seeker.

I am Philip R. Wyatt, the founder and director of Georgia Paranormal Investigations. I had the unexpected pleasure of meeting Heather Leigh several years ago, as we were both guest speakers on a paranormal discussion panel. Listening to her speak, I was instantly drawn to her like-minded thinking. She approaches the paranormal field with all the traits a great paranormal investigator needs: skepticism; a determination for truth-seeking, critical thinking, scientific and logical; and empathy for remembering that "ghosts" are people, too. As the media have conditioned us to see everything paranormal as evil, grotesque and something to be feared, Heather Leigh does not conform to that conditioning. This is when I became a fan of Heather Leigh. After that panel, I was lucky enough to call her a friend.

When 2020 hit us with the unprecedented pandemic of our lifetime, Heather Leigh and I saw the paranormal community losing touch with each other due to almost every paranormal event being canceled. This was when we came up with the idea of the Facebook live stream of *Ghost Education 101*—bringing our community together virtually while learning valuable information about our field through presentations and interviews with some of the most admired people in the paranormal world. We are now gratefully going into the fourth year of our podcast. I've witnessed Heather Leigh's dedication firsthand, cohosting our paranormal podcast. Each presentation and interview was tackled with meticulous research and a healthy dose of skepticism, yet always with that spark of belief in the unseen. That balance, that refusal to let cynicism extinguish the flame of curiosity, makes her such a compelling guide through this haunted paranormal world.

So turn the page, dear reader, and step into the world where shadows glare and the pounding of your heart echoes. Prepare to be unsettled and feel the chill and enduring power of long-told stories that refuse to be buried. Open that creaky door, turn down the lights and let Heather Leigh's words lead you down a moonlit path where every rustle might be a whisper; just be warned, you might never look at a dusty attic or a creaking floorboard the same way again.

And don't blame Heather Leigh if you start hearing whispers in your walls afterward.

—Philip R. Wyatt
Founder and director
Georgia Paranormal Investigations

ACKNOWLEDGEMENTS

I would like to express my deepest gratitude to the following individuals whose support and contributions have been invaluable in the creation of this book.

First and foremost, I am immensely grateful to Josh and Aidan, my husband and son (and members of Exploration Paranormal), whose guidance and wisdom have shaped this project (and my many other projects) from its inception. Your support, insights and assistance in researching and taking photos have been instrumental in bringing this work to fruition.

I extend my sincere appreciation to Philip R. Wyatt, who wrote an amazing foreword for this book. He has also been an amazing partner and co-host of *Ghost Education 101*.

My heartfelt thanks go to my family for their unwavering encouragement and understanding during the long hours spent in research and writing. Your love and support sustained me through the challenges of this journey.

To my friends and colleagues who offered moral support and valuable feedback, thank you for being a source of inspiration and motivation.

Lastly, I want to express my gratitude to the countless individuals who may not be mentioned here but have played a role, big or small, in shaping my journey as an author. This book would not have been possible without the collective effort and support of these incredible individuals. Thank you for being a part of this journey.

INTRODUCTION

When it comes to the wacky and weird, Florida has it all. From giant oranges to castles made of coral, the Sunshine State is home to some of the most bizarre and fascinating roadside attractions. Heck, the state is also home to "Florida Man," who is blamed for all sorts of weird activities and human behaviors.

Welcome to the Sunshine State, where the palm trees sway in the warm breeze and the sunsets paint the sky in hues of orange and pink. But beneath the veneer of tropical paradise lies a world shrouded in mystery, where the past refuses to rest in peace. In the following pages, I invite you to embark on a spine-tingling journey through the heart of Florida's most haunted roadside attractions.

With its rich history and diverse cultures, Florida has always been a magnet for the strange and unexplained. From the enigmatic swamps of the Everglades to the enchanting shores of Key West, the state is a tapestry of eerie tales and ghostly encounters. But it is along the highways and byways, at the quirky and charming roadside attractions, where the paranormal truly comes to life.

As you turn these pages, you'll encounter the restless spirits that linger at the forgotten motels, the phantoms that dance in the moonlight at amusement parks and the eerie tales of those who dared to explore the haunted lighthouses that dot the coastline. These stories aren't mere legends; they are the whispered secrets of Florida's past, stories passed down through generations, tales that continue to captivate and terrify those who dare to listen.

Florida's roadside attractions offer a unique glimpse into the supernatural realm, from the haunted halls of vintage diners to the ghostly apparitions that guard historic forts. Whether you're a seasoned paranormal enthusiast or a curious traveler seeking an unforgettable adventure, this book will guide you to the most haunted and intriguing destinations the Sunshine State offers.

So fasten your seatbelts and prepare to traverse the highways of the afterlife as we uncover the spine-chilling stories and unexplainable occurrences that haunt Florida's picturesque and peculiar roadside attractions. It's a journey into the unknown, where history, folklore and the supernatural collide in a way that can happen only in the land of perpetual sunshine and shadows. Welcome to *Haunted Florida Roadside Attractions*—where the past never lets go.

WHAT MAKES A FLORIDA ROADSIDE ATTRACTION?

By definition, a roadside attraction is a feature or uniquely constructed location set along the side of the road meant to attract tourists and offer a place for weary travelers to take a break. Some of the most popular roadside attractions in the United States include Cadillac Ranch, Carhenge, Cabazon Dinosaurs, the Fremont Troll, Corn Palace and more. The oldest roadside attraction in the United States is Lucy the Elephant, built in 1881 and beloved by those who travel through Margate City, New Jersey.

Long-distance travel was made possible in the 1920s as vehicle designs improved and more people purchased them. With road travel increasing, entrepreneurs started thinking and began constructing restaurants, coffee shops, cafés, motels and unusual businesses to attract travelers. In many cases, the buildings became attractive and were built in odd shapes or designs, such as ice cream cones, dinosaurs, spaceships and so on.

Some entrepreneurs designed their roadside attractions to be quick stops, allowing travelers to take a break from driving, grab something to eat, get some gas and head back out on the road. Others wanted to take more advantage of the increased traffic on highways and added hotels/motels and small attractions, such as monuments, illusionary amusements, museums of curiosities and areas to explore. These roadside attractions were designed to intrigue travelers, encouraging them to stick around the area for several hours, often spending the night before heading to their next destination.

There was a sudden spike in the popularity of roadside attractions after World War II. When soldiers returned home from war, they were excited to explore their country. As a way to spend time with the family, soldiers and their families packed up the car and hit the road.

The idea of roadside attractions continued to be widespread from the 1940s to the 1960s in the United States and Canada. Many years later, roadside attractions became popular among those taking road trips in Australia.

In most cases, roadside attractions serve as a stopping point while traveling, not the final destination. It is not uncommon to see roadside attractions advertised on billboards that fly by in the wink of an eye while driving along the highways.

Florida is home to more than one hundred roadside attractions, many scattered along highways such as Interstate 95, Interstate 4, Interstate 72, US 27 and Highway A1A. There are several more roadside attractions in

Opposite: Lucy the Elephant is a six-story elephant-shaped example of novelty architecture, constructed of wood and tin sheeting in 1881 by James V. Lafferty in Margate City, New Jersey, two miles south of Atlantic City. *Carol M. Highsmith, Library of Congress.*

Left, top: Billboard, Florida Alligator Farm, Route 301. *John Margolies, Library of Congress.*

Left, bottom: Alligator Farm, billboard 1, Route A1A, St. Augustine. *John Margolies, Library of Congress.*

the state that are no longer found on major highways because the highways of the past have been replaced with new roads, providing a more efficient means to travel cross-country.

WHY ARE ROADSIDE ATTRACTIONS HAUNTED?

Americans and foreign tourists love roadside attractions because they are educational, inspirational, hilarious, puzzling and haunted. With thousands of roadside attractions across the country, travelers can experience any travel adventure they desire. Several roadside attractions are creepy, run-down or abandoned, which makes them look and feel haunted.

Though many of these roadside attractions look and feel haunted, not all are. However, there are several that are haunted, and the reasons behind why they are haunted are often tied to the history of the location.

So, what are the reasons why so many roadside attractions are haunted? There is no single way to answer this question because it requires a more complex series of answers that may point to why a location is haunted.

The first reason is that many of these locations, especially the ones that are historical markers, identify locations where historic and tragic events occurred. Though this is a common belief as to why a location is haunted, the idea that something dark, terrifying or traumatic has to happen for a place to be haunted is a common misconception. While terrible events at locations such as battlefields or asylums can cause paranormal activity, this is not the sole reason for a place to become haunted.

Another reason is the location may have an extensive collection of historical objects, antiques and artifacts. These items may be what is causing the paranormal activity to occur. It is known that objects can act as a way for the dead to connect with the living, and in many cases, spirits become attached to objects, wanting to hang around where the item is

Top: A quirky (and at first glance fearsome) roadside attraction, so big that it takes both a truck and a trailer to hold him, at the St. Augustine Alligator Farm Zoological Park in St. Augustine. *Carol M. Highsmith, Library of Congress.*

Bottom: Part of a long-abandoned but mysteriously still nearly fully stocked Florida Souvenirland pecan, candy and souvenir location near Lawtey in Central Florida. *Carol M. Highsmith, Library of Congress.*

housed. Haunted objects are commonly found in museums, restaurants with memorabilia on the walls or roadside attractions displaying these items.

Another reason locations, including roadside attractions, can become haunted is that they are the sites where many people enjoy life. Roadside attractions are happy places where many people make memories with friends and family. Why wouldn't someone want to live their afterlife at a location where they were comfortable or content and experienced lots of joy?

Two other reasons why a location may be haunted include self-manifestation and summoning. Sometimes, people want an area to be haunted so that they can share stories and eventually self-manifest something paranormal. It is also possible that the spirits were summoned to the location, most commonly through rituals.

Though not all roadside attractions are haunted, it is safe to say that many are, which, for paranormal enthusiasts, makes them more exciting to visit.

Ripley's Believe It or Not!

St. Augustine

Ripley's Believe It or Not! is one of the most popular destinations in St. Augustine for travelers looking for a unique and odd experience. This location has something for everyone and is a roadside attraction requiring more than an hour or so to explore.

Visiting Ripley's Believe It or Not![1] grants visitors access to various artifacts, unique exhibits and odd interactives, including Red Train Tours, Mirror Mazes, LaseRaces, 3D Theaters and mini golf courses. The St. Augustine location also offers various haunted history experiences like no other location in Florida.

One haunted experience at Ripley's Believe It or Not! features an opportunity to learn about the nation's oldest city and its history. To experience the attraction's spirits up close, hop aboard the Red Train Tour to enjoy the sights on the way to visit the ghosts of Castle Warden during Ripley's Haunted Castle Investigation.

The Haunted Castle Investigation is the only St. Augustine tour that offers firsthand training with hands-on experience about what it is like being a paranormal investigator. Visitors are taken on an inside journey through what is often referred to as the most haunted building on the Southeastern Seaboard. This experience offers visitors a chance to encounter paranormal entities and the dark past of St. Augustine.

Ripley's Believe It or Not! is set inside an 1880s castle built by William G. Warden, one of the partners of Standard Oil. This building was later transformed into a hotel owned by *The Yearling* author Marjorie Kinnan

Top: The Ripley's Believe It or Not! tourist attraction in St. Augustine. *Carol M. Highsmith, Library of Congress.*

Bottom: Ripley's Believe It or Not! billboard, Route A1A. *John Margolies, Library of Congress.*

Rawlings and her husband, Norton Baskin. The couple owned the building before it was purchased by Ripley's and turned it into a place of all things strange, unusual and odd.

There are several theories behind why Ripley's Believe It or Not! is haunted. Though most of the paranormal activity happening at Ripley's is believed to be attached to the artifacts and displays, the building itself is also rumored to be haunted by its tragic past. Local legends claim that Ruth Hopkins Pickering and Betty Neville Richeson perished in a fire in 1944 but did not die directly from the fire. It is rumored the two women were murdered first, and then their bodies were burned by their attacker in an attempt to cover their tracks. The apparitions of these women have been spotted at the location, often peering out from the windows of their rooms.

Additionally, LeRoy Robert Ripley passed away in 1949 and was known to visit the hotel often before it became one of his famous museums. Even

Top: An unusual moose "trophy head" at the Ripley's Believe It or Not! tourist attraction in St. Augustine. *Carol M. Highsmith, Library of Congress.*

Middle: What the Ripley's Believe It or Not! tourist attraction in St. Augustine calls its "Nail Fetish Statue." *Carol M. Highsmith, Library of Congress.*

Bottom: A most unsettling tunnel of small, whirling lights at the Ripley's Believe It or Not! tourist attraction in St. Augustine. *Carol M. Highsmith, Library of Congress.*

A genuine shrunken head, an Ecuadorian wartime trophy, displayed at the Ripley's Believe It or Not! tourist attraction in St. Augustine. *Carol M. Highsmith, Library of Congress.*

though the St. Augustine museum was founded and opened after his death, his spirit has been seen walking the displays as if he remains behind to admire what his legacy has become.

The mummified cat on display at Ripley's Believe It or Not! Museum in St. Augustine has drawn much attention, especially among paranormal researchers. This artifact has been the topic of esoteric discussions and has attracted some "otherworldly" attention.

The shrunken human heads at Ripley's are more odd artifacts, and evidence from research and testing dates the shrunken heads back to prehistoric times. These heads are surrounded by tons of superstition and mystery among the Natives of Tsantsas. Not only are the shrunken heads eerily creepy, but many people feel a strange presence standing behind them when viewing the artifacts. Could this be the spirits of the bodies the heads originally belonged to? Or is the curse associated with the heads that linger over the museum? Either way, they are pretty gruesome.

Ripley's Believe It or Not! is one location in St. Augustine where the dead reveal themselves to the living when the sun sets. This roadside attraction is definitely one where the strange, bizarre and unexpected meet reality.

SPOOK HILL

LAKE WALES

Spook Hill is one of Florida's most iconic paranormal roadside attractions and is conveniently located about fifty miles south of Walt Disney World. Many legends and mystical stories are tied to this quiet area of Lake Wales, and it is often referred to as a magnetic hill, an anti-gravity location or a gravity hill.

Spook Hill is not the only gravity hill in the world, but it is one of the country's oldest gravity hills and the only one in Florida.[2] There are hundreds around the world, and this one became so popular in Florida that the City of Lake Wales reached out and acquired the rights to use Casper the Friendly Ghost as the mascot of the nearby school, Spook Hill Elementary.[3]

In theory, when a vehicle is placed in neutral on a gravity hill, such as Spook Hill, it will appear as if it is rolling uphill. The hill's qualities caused trouble before cars were invented. Horses would find it challenging and struggle to walk downhill in this area.

The Florida legend behind why Spook Hill is such an intriguing place claims an alligator terrorized a local village. The village's Indian chief sought out and fought this alligator in an intense fight, resulting in the death of the chief and the alligator. The chief was buried on the north side of the hill, and some claim he remains behind to watch over the area protecting it.

From here, different legends offer stories about who or what haunts Spook Hill. It is unknown if it is the alligator or the Indian chief haunting the hill, causing vehicles to roll the wrong way up the hill. But in all reality, though their spirits may be haunting the hill, neither is responsible for the anti-

One could drive their car to the bottom of the "hill," turn off the engine, release the brakes and watch as the car rolled back as much as one hundred feet up the hill. This is due to an optical illusion. *State Archives of Florida.*

gravity effects experienced when on the hill. The hill's effects result from a peculiar optical illusion, making it feel like the vehicle is rolling uphill when it is actually rolling downhill.

In the 1950s, during the golden age of America's roadside attractions, Spook Hill grew in popularity, and many locals started building businesses, including restaurants, hotels and shops, to meet the demands of visitors coming to the area to experience the hill's anti-gravity effects in person.

Barney's Tavern in Lake Wales created a leaflet with information about another popular legend surrounding the phenomenon on Spook Hill. The pamphlet is titled "The Real Story Behind Spook Hill" and was handed out to many people who passed through town.

The alternative legend behind the mystery of Spook Hill involves a story about two pirates, Teniente Vanilla and Captain Gimme Sarsaparilla, who spent years pillaging and plundering on the high seas. The two, who made Tampa's José Gaspar look like an ordinary freebooter, decided to retire in

Left: A car riding along Spook Hill in Lake Wales. *State Archives of Florida.*

Below: A car rolling "up" the Spook Hill attraction in Lake Wales. *State Archives of Florida.*

Lake Wales. Legend has it that when Vanilla died, he was buried at the foot of Spook Hill, while Captain Sarsaparilla ended up at the bottom of Lake Wales.

Continuing with the legend, centuries later, a man wanted to go fishing in the area and parked his car at the bottom of Spook Hill. While he was walking toward his fishing spot, the vehicle started traveling backward uphill. It seemed the car was moving even when the engine was shut off. The man cried out, "Dem's spooks!" before he fainted; according to the leaflets, this is how Spook Hill got its name.

"Greetings from Spook Hill"

Above: Greetings from Spook Hill. *State Archives of Florida.*

Left: Spook Hill attraction in Lake Wales. *State Archives of Florida.*

This page: Spook Hill today, where many cars still make a stop to see if the legend is real. *Heather Leigh, PhD.*

So if this legend is true, why do cars roll up the hill?

The legend claims the man parked his car on top of Vanilla's unmarked grave, causing him to wake from his slumber. Calling out for help, Sarsaparilla rose from his underwater grave to push the car to his friend's final resting spot. To this day, Sarsaparilla's spirit comes to Vanilla's rescue, driving any vehicle that stops on his unmarked grave.

Other theories about why vehicles act as they do on Spook Hill include mole people, the skunk ape (Florida's Bigfoot), underground magnets and aliens.

SKUNK APE RESEARCH HEADQUARTERS

OCHOPEE

The skunk ape is a sasquatch-like creature known for roaming the Everglades and other heavily wooded areas of Florida. Though several people have reportedly come face to face with Florida's version of Bigfoot, several people dismiss these sightings as if they are seeing some large animal, such as a bear.

Despite so many people dismissing the idea of the skunk ape, brothers Dave and Jack Shealy founded the Skunk Ape Research Headquarters in Ochopee. The research center is a museum, gift shop and wildlife attraction on the edge of the Everglades along the Tamiami Trail.

Dave Shealy, who has studied the skunk ape all his life, describes these creatures as six to seven feet tall, weighing between 350 and 450 pounds. It is believed that between seven and nine skunk apes are hanging around the boggy wetlands and towering sawgrass.

This creature mostly hides beneath alligator dens, often filled with swamp gas and animal carcasses. Exposure to these items and the animal's lack of bathing creates the horrific smell many claim to sense when the skunk ape is near.

Several reports have been made associated with sightings of the skunk ape, and in the '70s and '80s, the number of sightings started to pick up. Explorers of the Florida Everglades share stories of smelling the creature, coming face to face and spotting footprints on the muddy shores. Though rare, some witnesses have captured images of the skunk ape in video and still photography shots.

When visiting the Skunk Ape Research Headquarters, there is a significant chance that you may run into this smelly bipedal creature, especially if you plan to venture into the Everglades. Just don't travel too far into the Everglades, because there have been several reports of people going into this region of Florida and never coming out.

ROBERT THE DOLL AT EAST MARTELLO MUSEUM

KEY WEST

The story of Robert the Doll is one of the most fascinating stories from the Sunshine State and is one of the state's top attractions, especially among those wanting to experience all things odd and spooky. Robert the Doll is a famous resident living at the East Martello Museum in Key West, offering visitors a skin-crawling front-row look at the doll and his small canine friend.

Robert the Doll is tied to a young boy who received the doll believed to have been manufactured by the Steiff Company of Germany in the early 1900s. His grandfather purchased the doll while in Germany in 1904 on a trip and gave it to Robert Eugene Otto as a birthday gift. The doll's sailor outfit is likely one that young Robert Eugene wore as a child.

An alternative story about where the one-of-a-kind, handmade doll came from is that it was given to the boy as a birthday gift by one of the family's servants. Another similar legend is that a young girl of Bahamian descent gave the doll to the Otto boy as a gift or retaliation for the family's wrongdoing.

When Robert Eugene Otto received the doll, strange and cursed occurrences happened inside the Otto home.

Over the years, Robert Eugene Otto insisted on being called Eugene or Gene, and the doll was to be called Robert. The boy claimed it was the doll who insisted on the name change. Many odd things happened in Otto's home, including objects being broken and things moving around and the

Robert the Doll. *Photo by Rob O'Neal.*

doll being found in locations such as other rooms from where it was left. Whenever Gene was punished for breaking something, he often claimed, "Robert did it."

Gene grew up and moved on with his life, but the thought of Robert remained a prominent figure in the back of his mind. Even though he moved away to study art in New York and Paris, he returned to the Otto family home in Key West after getting married to Annette Parker in Paris on May 3, 1930. They lived there until he died in 1974, and his wife died two years later.

After the couple died, their Eaton Street home in Key West was sold to Myrtle Reuter, who owned the home that was sold to her with Robert the Doll inside. She held the home for twenty years until the new owners purchased the property to use as a guest house.

Because of the legend and its unique design, Robert the Doll was donated to the East Martello Museum in Key West in 1994. After finding his new residence, the doll became an overnight sensation and a popular tourist attraction.

According to legend, Robert the Doll has supernatural abilities, allowing him to move, change facial expressions and create giggling sounds. Several stories claim the doll could move figurines around the room, and he was very aware of what was happening around him. Some believe that the wrongdoings of Robert the Doll were self-manifestations of the young boy's consistent need to blame the doll for everything he was getting in trouble for.

Though there were many signs indicating that the doll may have been possessed, the first true hint that something was out of the ordinary occurred one night when Gene woke up to find Robert the Doll staring at him on the edge of his bed. Gene was only ten then, and he started screaming

East Martello Tower, old Spanish fort, Key West. *Arthur Rothstein, Library of Congress.*

for help. His mother was awakened by his screaming and furniture being overturned in Gene's room. She struggled to open the door and panicked when hearing her son begging for help.

Finally, when she could open the door, she saw her son curled up in fear on his bed, his room in shambles and the doll peacefully sitting at the foot of the bed. All Gene could say was, "Robert did it."

Though it was common for Gene to blame Robert for the many strange occurrences happening in the home, it is still uncertain if it was the doll or the child blaming the doll for his naughty behavior. However, it was common for Gene's parents to hear him talking to the doll upstairs, and they would listen to a response in a different voice. Additionally, his parents reported seeing Robert the Doll speak and witnessed his various changes in facial expressions. Other strange occurrences include hearing Robert the Doll giggle, seeing him run up the stairs and spotting him staring out of the upstairs window.

Later on, Gene's wife Ann had an uneasy feeling about having Robert in the house, and though she could never put her finger on the root cause of the feeling, she still insisted Gene lock the doll up in the attic. Gene finally gave in to his wife's wishes, and Robert the Doll was unhappy with the decision to seclude him in the attic. When friends and family would come over to the home, they could hear footsteps in the attic, as if someone was pacing back and forth. Devilish giggling could also be heard coming from the attic.

Neighbors reported seeing Robert sitting in the window watching over them, and the local children claimed to see the doll moving as if it were mocking them as they walked to school. Some neighbors told Gene that they

34

had seen the doll sitting by the window in the upstairs bedroom, which was odd to him because he knew he had locked Robert in the attic. When he investigated, he found Robert in the rocking chair beside the window. Gene moved Robert back to the attic, locking him in several times, and each time, he would later discover him sitting in the bedroom rocking chair.

Even after Gene's death in 1974, Robert continued his rampage of paranormal terror. The new owner of the home on Eaton Street claimed their ten-year-old daughter was first delighted to find the doll in the attic but quickly became terrified. She claimed the doll was alive and would hurt her. One night, the daughter woke up screaming in fear, and when her parents rushed to the room, she said that Robert had moved about the room.

It didn't take the new owners long to get rid of Robert the Doll, and he eventually ended up in the hands of those running the museum at the East Martello Fort.

To this day, Robert the Doll has been blamed for many things, including auto accidents, broken bones, economic struggles, job loss, divorce and a cornucopia of other misfortunes. Several people believe their misfortunes after leaving the museum resulted from their not fully respecting Robert the Doll.

Even though Robert the Doll sits behind plexiglass at the East Martello Tower Museum, several visitors have seen him change his expression. Some have even heard a child's giggle behind their backs when in the same room as the doll. Some museum staff members have even seen Robert put his hand against the glass of his case.

Legend claims he does not like his photo taken, and if you do not ask for permission or if he is not in the mood, he is known to curse those he feels betray his wishes. Several people have written letters apologizing to Robert the Doll, hoping to free themselves from his curse because they

Entrance to the East Martello Tower Museum in Key West, which is home to Robert the Doll. *Dale McDonald, State Archives of Florida.*

either didn't ask permission to take his photo or made fun of the doll during their visit.

Most people continue to speak about Robert the Doll as if he is a person and not a doll. It is expected to feel like someone is watching when visiting this Key West museum, especially in the same room as Robert the Doll.

Other paranormal activities experienced when in the presence of Robert the Doll include feeling some unseen force touch their knee, seeing lights flickering and cameras malfunctioning, especially when Robert does not want his picture taken.

When visiting Robert the Doll, be polite and don't forget to ask permission to take his photograph. Otherwise, you may be writing a letter to him asking for forgiveness.

PLEASE NOTE: There are many rumors about Zak Bagans retaining ownership of Robert the Doll in the Haunted Museum in Las Vegas, Nevada, which are false. Robert the Doll was at his museum for the filming of *Deadly Possessions*. However, Bagans did not purchase the doll, nor does it reside at his museum. Robert happily lives in Key West, soaking up the Florida sunshine and residing at the East Martello Tower Museum.

CASSADAGA SPIRITUALIST CAMP

CASSADAGA

Cassadaga is a quiet community between Orlando and Daytona, founded in the late 1800s. Founded as the Cassadaga Spiritualist Camp, it has more than one hundred residents today, including several psychics and mediums. Several people, including residents, have referred to Cassadaga as the town "where Mayberry meets the Twilight Zone."

Meaning "Water Beneath the Rocks" in the Seneca Indian language, Cassadaga is known for being home to renowned psychics and mediums. Several times, publications have referred to the town as the "Psychic Capital of the World."

In 1875, George P. Colby, a trance medium from Pike, New York, founded the Southern Cassadaga Spiritualist Meeting Association. At the same time, the Cassadaga Spiritualist Camp was born. Today, the town welcomes visitors for readings and opportunities to learn more about those living in the area.

The entire town is a popular roadside attraction in Florida, especially among those seeking spiritual guidance or new-age books, crystals and dream catchers. The community offers visits with an officially certified medium and opportunities to have your aura read or roam the area's woods.

The Cassadaga Camp is a popular roadside attraction, offering visitors access to a welcome center, the Colby Memorial Temple, a community library, the Cassadaga Hotel, a central auditorium and a camp bookstore. The town is also home to the Caesar Forman Healing Center and the Andrew Jackson Davis Educational Building, used for gatherings and musical performances.

Above: Cassadaga Hotel. *Mary Lou Norwood, State Archives of Florida.*

Opposite: Entrance to Camp Cassadaga, Lake Helen. *State Archives of Florida.*

Spiritualism was a movement based on the belief that spirits can communicate with the living. Often, this communication is through mediums, but it can also be done using various methods, including seances, spirit board sessions and paranormal investigations. Ultimately, Spiritualism identifies the ability and means to communicate with those living on the other side of life.

Cassadaga is the place to go when looking for additional information, help with and training in Spiritualism. Spirits flock to the area hoping to communicate with the living, knowing this community has the means and the desire to establish meaningful conversations between the living and the dead.

But be careful. The woods and the famous Cassadaga Hotel are rumored to be haunted, as former guests remain behind checking in as new guests arrive.

Hotel Cassadaga is a two-story property not affiliated with the Spiritualist camp but is a must-visit when exploring the area. One of the most commonly reported paranormal experiences is hearing children running up and down the hotel hallways, playing and laughing. Sounds of tricycle bells are also heard ringing through the hallways. These must be the sounds of spirits

visiting the hotel because children cannot stay overnight.

The Cassadaga Hotel is also home to the friendly spirit of a former night clerk named Arthur, who makes an appearance by reporting to work. Like the other spirits at the hotel, Arthur remains behind, watching over the hotel, keeping it safe and protected.

The spirit of Gentleman Jack also hangs out at the hotel smoking cigars and hitting on the ladies. Additionally, the spirits of Kaitlin and Sarah are two young ladies who also like to spend their afterlife at the Cassadaga Hotel.

Across the street from the hotel is C. Green's Haunted History House & Museum, home to many haunted dolls, a haunted Ouija board collection, historical photographs and artifacts. The museum is also home to George Colby's original seance table.

In addition to the Cassadaga Hotel being haunted, the Ann Stevens House, a short walk from the town's historic district, is rumored to be the home of two vortexes. This ten-room home is split between the main house and a carriage house, built in 1895 by Ann Stevens, one of the first Spiritualists to settle in Cassadaga.

Today, the Ann Stevens House is a bed-and-breakfast and is rumored to be visited by the spirits of a little girl named Marjorie and Virgil, a gardener who lived near the home. Residents and visitors have seen these two spirits. Local psychics say a doll within the house belonged to Marjorie and now sits in a little chair in the bed-and-breakfast parlor.

The property of the bed-and-breakfast contains two vortexes along hiking trails within the property, which causes a pendulum placed over the vortex to start frantically spinning for no reason. The vortexes are typically only accessible to guests staying on the property, but these areas are open to the public on special days.

Cassadaga is home to the Devil's Chair, offering visitors a place to hang out and chill when exploring the cemetery. The cemetery contains many tombstones from the 1800s belonging to early Spiritualists, including a

Main Street with a sign for mediums, Cassadaga. *Mary Lou Norwood, State Archives of Florida.*

graveside brick wall with a bench created as a nineteenth-century memorial sculpture known as the Devil's Chair.

Local legend maintains that anyone who takes a seat in the Devil's Chair risks finding themselves visited by the devil himself in the near future. Additionally, if an unopened can of beer is left on the bench, it will be empty (without it being opened) by morning and believed to have been drunk by the devil. Though this chair is meant to be nothing but a monument and a place to sit when visiting loved ones in the cemetery, several legends have turned the brick chair into an attraction taunting those wanting to press their luck in an attempt to see the devil.

A short walk from the welcome center is the Fairy Trail and Horseshoe Park, a beautiful area to stroll in and believed to be full of manifestations and natural spirits. Throughout the woods, you will encounter figurines of a gnome, a toadstool and a fairy, among other statues and decorations. Several visitors have seen light anomalies floating through the wooded areas and feel their inner child emerge as they experience a boost of child-like energy.

Cassadaga is home to many unique activities and is one place to visit in Florida when looking to encounter multiple spirits. Since the community has various spirits and entities residing in and visiting the town, there is always the chance of meeting everything, from fun fairies to the devil himself.

FOUNTAIN OF YOUTH
ARCHAEOLOGICAL PARK

ST. AUGUSTINE

The oldest city in the United States holds the key to living forever. At least, that is what one roadside attraction in St. Augustine claims to possess.

Visiting the Fountain of Youth today provides more than just a stop to see a majestic fountain with a unique history. This roadside attraction showcases what Spanish settlements were like and is home to a planetarium and many exhibits, including blacksmith and historic firearms exhibits.

For centuries, explorers have been searching for the source of eternal life, and Juan Ponce de Leon believed he had discovered it when he stumbled upon the legend of the Fountain of Youth in St. Augustine. However, some believe that what he found was not the Fountain of Youth, and his explorations failed to uncover the fountain's location.

Legends claim those who visit the healing waters of the fountain can magically maintain a youthful appearance, and if they drink from the spring's waters, they can increase their chances of living forever. The myth holding the idea that the fountain contains magical powers linked to eternal youth is tied to a Taino Indian legend that the spring existed on the island of Bimini, and the area became known as Florida; it was believed to restore the youth of those who bathed in the refreshing spring waters.

Ponce de Leon settled in the New World in search of gold and riches for Spain, claiming La Florida for his mother country. After Ponce de Leon arrived in Florida from Spain in 1513, he discovered the New World already had an extensive history dating back long before his arrival. Several

Top: Fountain of Youth billboard, Route A1A. *John Margolies, Library of Congress.*

Bottom: Statue of Juan Ponce de Leon in St. Augustine. *Carol M. Highsmith, Library of Congress.*

archaeological discoveries found that the Timucua inhabited the area of St. Augustine for about three thousand years before Europeans came to the land. The Timucuans lived off their natural surroundings, surviving by hunting with bows and arrows, fishing from land and handcrafted canoes and cultivating corn and pumpkins.

Upon their arrival, Spanish explorers were served a celebration meal crafted from the food provisions stocked on their ship. They invited the Timucua Indians to join the feast, known as the first Thanksgiving feast in the New World. This Thanksgiving was hosted on September 8, 1565, fifty-six years before the meal with the Pilgrims of Plymouth.

Top: Entrance to the Fountain of Youth Archaeological Park in St. Augustine. *Carol M. Highsmith, Library of Congress.*

Bottom: Fountain of Youth, St. Augustine. *Frances Benjamin Johnston, Library of Congress.*

The Fountain of Youth Archaeological Park has been part of Florida's tourism since the 1860s, when the area started as a small series of attractions. These attractions showcased the spring and the grounds' breathtaking beauty. Luella Day "Diamond Lil" McConnell expanded the attraction by fabricating stories about the fountain to amuse and appall residents and tourists until she unexpectedly died in 1927.

The attraction was purchased by Walter B. Fraser in 1927. Originally from Georgia, Fraser relocated to Florida after the purchase and became significantly involved in local politics. He was the forerunner for a preservation program, organizing St. Augustine's first formal restoration

This page: Fountain of Youth, Indian Burial Ground, St. Augustine. *Frances Benjamin Johnston, Library of Congress.*

movement and developing the Historic St. Augustine Preservation Board in the 1930s.

In 1934, when excavation began, more than one hundred skeletal human remains were discovered. These remains were believed to have been buried using Christian methods and rituals, indicating when the first Christian Indians lived in the area. Smithsonian archaeologists were called to evaluate the remains, and they were carefully relocated to a nearby Christian cemetery using another religious burial ceremony.

Several visitors claim to have witnessed the presence of Ponce de Leon when exploring the area around the Fountain of Youth. The spirit of a man dressed like the Spanish conquistador has been spotted near the statue of a man sitting in the Plaza de La Constitución. Though de Leon's spirit has been spotted in other parts of Florida, many believe he still haunts the area around the Fountain of Youth because he was obsessed with discovering the fountain and the idea of the legend that continues to evade his discovery.

Those living on the Florida coast in and around St. Augustine have also reported seeing ghost ships sailing in the Atlantic with Spanish flags flying. It is believed these ghost ships disappear into the mist as they search the coastline for hints of where the Fountain of Youth is located.

PONCE INLET LIGHTHOUSE AND MUSEUM

PONCE INLET

The Ponce Inlet Lighthouse and Museum is a popular destination among lighthouse enthusiasts, especially those including Florida in their upcoming road trip itinerary. Nestled on the Ponce Inlet, this lighthouse is about one hour south of St. Augustine, making this 1887 lighthouse, which is Florida's tallest lighthouse, an easy trip when visiting the major roadside attractions in the state's oldest city.

The Ponce Inlet Lighthouse and Museum was constructed in 1887, and today, it offers visitors an opportunity to step back in time as they climb the 175 feet of the lighthouse tower. The lighthouse initially operated with a kerosene lamp, but the light was replaced with a fixed Fresnel lens. The lighthouse has guided mariners along Florida's east coast and was declared a National Historic Landmark in 1998.

Set on what was originally called the Mosquito Inlet, the first lighthouse on the inlet was erected in 1835. However, this lighthouse experienced many challenges, including the lamp's oil never arriving. Then, soon after tower construction was completed, the area suffered severe damage from a strong storm, which washed much of the sand from around the tower's base, weakening the structure.

In December 1835, Seminole Indians attacked the lighthouse as a strategic maneuver during the Second Seminole War. During the attack, glass in the lantern room was smashed, and the wooden stairs were set on fire.

After the attack, the lighthouse keeper and other locals left the area abandoned and unattended. The ongoing war prevented the necessary

Ponce de Leon Inlet Lighthouse, Ponce Inlet. *Carol M. Highsmith, Library of Congress.*

upkeep and repairs to correct the storm damage, leading to the tower's eventual collapse the following year.

Author and journalist Stephen Crane was aboard the SS *Commodore* when it sank off the coast in 1897. Luckily, he escaped death by riding a small dinghy with several crew members who found safety by seeking the Mosquito Inlet Light. He shared his experiences in the short story "The Open Boat."

The name was changed to Ponce de Leon Inlet in 1927, and the lighthouse was transferred from the Lighthouse Service to the United States Coast Guard in 1939. In 1970, the Coast Guard abandoned the lighthouse property, deeding it to the Town of Ponce Inlet.

The lighthouse grounds contain the answers to the area's historic past, and many believe the spirits of former lighthouse keepers and those who braved the ocean waters aboard Cuban rafts roam the area.

Even with living near Daytona, lighthouse keepers and their families led solitary, lonely lives at the Ponce Inlet Lighthouse. There were a few suicides and illnesses associated with living a life of isolation at the lighthouse. The lonely life and troubles that come with it have left a significant imprint on the area, and many believe the former keepers and their families haunt the surrounding land.

Two homes on the property are full of spirits, including one believed to be a keeper's wife or one of the female lighthouse keepers. Several people claim to have felt an unseen force touch their shoulder, hear disembodied voices and spot shadow figures darting throughout the rooms of these homes.

There is a third house currently glassed off, and visitors claim a weird-looking china doll has something attached to it. People feel uneasy in this home, see light anomalies and witness the doll moving when taking a series of photographs.

Top: Aerial view looking west at the Ponce de Leon Inlet Lighthouse near New Smyrna Beach. *State Archives of Florida.*

Bottom: Ponce de Leon Inlet Lighthouse. *State Archives of Florida.*

Though not many people believe the lighthouse tower to be haunted, there are several reports about encounters with a former assistant lighthouse keeper. The spirit of Joseph Davis remained behind at the lighthouse after the heart attack he suffered while working in 1919. Several people have smelled the presence of kerosene, which is believed to be connected to Davis's spirit. Though some residual scents could be left behind, kerosene has not been kept at the lighthouse since 1933.

The spirit of a former lighthouse keeper's son is also believed to haunt the lighthouse tower. The boy died after being kicked by a horse on the property. Several people have encountered this spirit playing pranks and opening and closing doors. Several light anomalies have also been spotted in the Ponce Inlet Lighthouse tower.

SUNKEN GARDENS

ST. PETERSBURG

For more than one hundred years, the Sunken Gardens in St. Petersburg has been offering travelers an exciting roadside attraction, making it the country's oldest one. The gardens are home to over fifty thousand plants and flowers of all tropical varieties. It is the perfect place to wander and explore pathways by gardens and waterfalls, including an area with pink flamingos. Sunken Gardens is the ideal roadside oasis for the living and the spirits behind haunting Sunken Gardens.

George Turner Sr., a plumber, purchased 4.1 acres of land in 1902 that would eventually be transformed into the world-famous botanical roadside attraction.[4] He used an elaborate maze of clay tiles to drain the ancient lake, revealing a rich muck soil ideal for his gardening hobby. He planted tropical fruit trees, including mangoes, bananas, papayas and guavas, selling the fruits from his family's abundant harvests at their fruit stand.

Once his garden was lush and thriving, Turner's neighbors enjoyed visiting and strolling through it. In the early 1930s, he started charging fifteen cents for tours of his gardens. He and his wife, Eula Turner, maintained the garden, establishing the grounds for the historic landmark it is today. Their children and grandchildren continued the family tradition, updating the gardens into a tropical oasis with refreshing flowing ponds.

Sunken Gardens officially opened as a roadside attraction to the public in 1936, providing travelers with the perfect place to rest in a subtropical oasis amid city life.

Alligator wrestler Paul Strazzula wrestles with ease at Florida's Sunken Gardens show in St. Petersburg. *Carol M. Highsmith, Library of Congress.*

Unfortunately, when theme parks, such as Walt Disney World and Universal Studios Orlando, became popular vacation destinations, attendance at old Florida attractions, including Sunken Gardens, dropped. The Turner family decided to sell the property in 1999, and the City of

St. Petersburg purchased it. The city continues to operate and manage the attraction, keeping it open every day of the week for the public to explore.

Sunken Gardens is nestled below sea level, which has created a disorienting landscape with an eerie feeling, skewed auras and a sensation of something unnatural. The odd feelings many experience have led to various legends and myths associated with the gardens. Beware when exploring the winding and labyrinthine trails because you may be surrounded by more than pink flamingos, tortoises and butterflies. Visitors have reported feeling like someone is watching or following them while they are walking through the gardens. Others have spotted darting shadow figures from the corners of their eyes, and when they take a closer look, they realize they are alone.

Whether it is the feeling many people experience while exploring the gardens that is self-manifesting paranormal activity within or the spirits of the founder and his family who look over the gardens in the afterlife, something strange is happening.

CORAL CASTLE MUSEUM

HOMESTEAD

C oral Castle is a unique attraction built solely by Edward Leedskalnin, a Latvian eccentric who used more than 1,100 tons of coral rock to build the site, mainly under moonlight. Leedskalnin weighed in at a mere 100 pounds and stood just over five feet tall, which led many to wonder how this man could have moved the chunks of coral into place without the assistance of others.

During the construction of Coral Castle, no one ever witnessed Leedskalnin working on his beloved building, and they never saw anyone else working on the structure. Because of this, several community members believed Leedskalnin to have supernatural powers or to have had the assistance of alien intelligence to build the castle. It took him twenty-eight years to build the castle, and he refused to allow anyone to witness his efforts or assist with the construction. When asked how he built Coral Castle, he would reply that he knew the secrets used by those who made the ancient pyramids and that if he could do it, anyone could do it. Some teenagers witnessed Leedskalnin at work, claiming he used hydrogen balloons to move the large chunks of coral. However, the only advanced tool he spoke of using was a "perpetual motion holder."

Coral Castle was constructed around 1923 and was initially named "Ed's Place." The first location for the castle was in Florida City, and it remained bordering the Florida Everglades until about 1936. Leedskalnin decided to relocate the castle north to its current location outside Homestead.

This page and opposite: Coral Castle, Homestead. *John Margolies, Library of Congress.*

Upon the castle's relocation, Leedskalnin renamed the property "Rock Gate" after the rear swinging gate he built into the brick wall. Under the cover of night, he continued work on the castle in its new location until he died in 1951. The newer coral pieces quarried after the property's move were collected only a few feet from the castle's walls. The pool and pit along the southern walls remain coral quarries, and the east and west quarries have been filled in.

It is uncertain what path ownership of the property took after Leedskalnin's death, but since he had no will, it was given to his closest living relative, his nephew Harry from Michigan. Since his nephew was in poor health, he sold the property to a family from Illinois in 1953. However, this information varies from the obituary of Julius Levin, a former Coral Castle owner who states he purchased the land from the State of Florida in 1952. It is rumored he didn't even know a castle was on the property.

Regardless of when or how Levin acquired the property, he turned it into a tourist attraction. The name changed from Rock Gate to Rock Gate Park and later to Coral Castle. In January 1981, Levin sold the property to Coral Castle, Inc., and it was listed on the National Register of Historic Places in 1984.

One of the most mysterious features of Coral Castle is the nine-ton gate that easily moves with the touch of a finger. This gate is so perfectly balanced that it is easy to carry while in place, but if it were to be removed, it would take six men and a fifty-short-ton crane to move it. Other popular features include the Polaris telescope, sundial, fountain and functioning rocking chairs made entirely of stone.

One of the most common misconceptions about Coral Castle is that the structure was built out of coral when it was actually built using oolite limestone. Oolite limestone is commonly found throughout southern Florida, typically under a small layer of topsoil, and is easily quarried.

Some of the mystery behind Coral Castle comes from the fact that no one saw Leedskalnin construct the castle, which led to several theories. One of the most commonly shared theories behind this man's greatest accomplishment is he had help from alien technology. Some believed this theory and thought it true because he preferred to work in the secrecy of night's darkness. Other theories include supernatural abilities, psychic powers, singing to the stones and a natural ability to use ancient sciences. Some people believe Coral Castle is positioned perfectly on the Earth's natural harmonic grid, which could have helped Leedskalnin with his magnetism, levitation and electrical current ability. He was known to conduct electrical experiments, and this could have been the perfect location for such experiments.

There is no doubt Coral Castle is haunted. When the sun sets and the crew locks up for the night, there are rumors the castle's property is overrun with supernatural entities, including aliens, vampires, transdimensional deities, angels, werewolves, pixies, demons and fairies. There is no shortage of creative legends behind who or what is haunting the Coral Castle.

Being close to the Bermuda Triangle, Coral Castle is believed to be visited by aliens. Some have referred to the property as a pit stop for UFOs, and several locals have reported seeing little green and gray men and massive UFOs hovering over the castle. The stone throne is believed to represent the seats used by alien pilots to control their ships.

At night, several people have reported seeing fireballs and light anomalies in nearby tree lines, and cameras have been known to malfunction during the day. When film cameras were used, many people who developed their film saw a strange figure or specter in the shot when no one was there.

Coral Castle staff members have reported hearing frightening shrieks and screams from various areas of the property.

The spirit of Leedskalnin is the most recognizable in the area and is often seen before dawn looking at his kingdom and taking measurements. Because he repeats the same activities, it is believed Leedskalnin's spirit is residual energy created by his repetitive actions during the construction of Coral Castle.

In addition to ghosts and aliens, Coral Castle has been known to attract native wildlife, including Florida panthers, gators and other apex predators. Still, it is also rumored that creatures such as the skunk ape have been spotted in the habitat surrounding the castle.

Legends surrounding Coral Castle include stories about the fae, including fairies, pixies and hobgoblins. Stories about the fae vary significantly in different regions of the world. For example, in the United States, many people see fairies as Tinker Bell or cute little winged creatures there to help us with their innocent magic. Europe, the home of fairy legends, features fairies as mischievous creatures who are sinister tricksters and bloodthirsty. Some stories make Jack the Ripper look like Winnie the Pooh.

Coral Castle is believed to be a favorite hunting ground for the fae, and there have been several reports of strange, small, elf-like creatures prowling among the massive stone structures. Some people have reported hearing high-pitched chattering from within the castle walls when no one is believed to be on the property.

Some people believe that Coral Castle is a location for all things supernatural and a wendigo or wraith haunts the land. Several visitors have reported hearing the call of the wendigo from the woods near the castle.

Dowsing rods are a popular and effective tool for exploring Coral Castle. Dowsers have detected an unusual energy flowing through the property, and some have revealed vortexes within the castle's boundaries.

It is safe to say that something paranormal is happening at Coral Castle, and it appears this roadside attraction attracts people worldwide—and some otherworldly creatures too.

Bok Tower Gardens

Lake Wales

L ake Wales is home to another popular roadside attraction that travelers can visit for a relaxing afternoon among beautiful gardens. Bok Tower Gardens opened in 1929 and has delighted visitors traveling between Orlando and Tampa. The most iconic features at this attraction include the Singing Tower carillon, the beautifully landscaped gardens and the impressive 1930s Mediterranean-style mansion.

The founder, Edward W. Bok, worked hard and would not settle for anything less than impressive when creating Bok Tower Gardens. When he came to Lake Wales from Pennsylvania to avoid the harsh winters, he fell in love with Florida's sunsets, birds and hills. His passion for these items contributed to his vision of creating a beautiful place where he hoped to inspire others.

To make his vision a reality, Bok worked with Frederick Law Olmsted Jr., a landscape architect, to create the Singing Tower, reflection pool and gardens. Once completed, he presented this roadside attraction as a gift to America to show appreciation for the many opportunities the country had presented him.

Bok Tower Gardens has nearly fifty acres with paved walking paths that wind through the beautiful gardens and among seasonal flowers. This is one of the best places in Florida to take a break and enjoy watching the colorful birds and wildlife—and possibly encounter a ghost or two.

Many people have reported an eerie feeling while admiring the beautiful Bok Tower and claim they feel like they are not alone when wandering the

Historic Bok Tower, Lake Wales. *Carol M. Highsmith, Library of Congress.*

meticulously manicured pathways. Some have reported seeing someone standing on the other side of the grounds, and as they walk closer, the figure gradually fades until the person disappears.

Are the spirits attracted to the beautiful gardens or the unique sounds coming from the Singing Tower? No one knows, but many claim Bok Tower Gardens is home to at least one spirit.

Silver Springs State Park

Silver Springs

Silver Springs is best known for its glass-bottom boat tours, and tourists worldwide travel to Florida to experience the adventure that awaits them at the Historic Silver Springs State Park. This roadside attraction has been a popular tourist destination since the 1870s, offering visitors guided tours, hiking, paddling and camping opportunities. The park has vast natural areas and tons of wildlife, including deer, alligators, turtles, manatees, birds and monkeys. Silver Springs State Park encompasses four thousand acres, including the springs, surrounding sandhill forest and the entire five-mile Silver River. Visitors can explore the winding trails set among serene gardens and historic structures.

Several ghost stories come from Silver Springs, many showing up in books and blogs and developing into urban legends. Over the years, as the stories have been shared from one person to another, several stories have warped, making the narrative scarier than the original story. Many stories have been forgotten, and several new stories have developed based on personal experiences and the legends behind the Silver Springs ghost stories.

Several stories are shared by those who work at Silver Springs, sharing their experiences coming face to face with the paranormal entities that call this park home. Some of the legends of Silver Springs are more poetic than others, and some are more believable than others. The best thing is you, as the reader, can decide which paranormal story and legend you like best.

One of the most famous ghostly legends from Silver Springs is also a story about two lovers. Aunt Silla, a woman who worked at the park, knew the two

This page: Silver Spring and Silver Spring Run. *George Barker, Library of Congress.*

young lovers and enjoyed sitting at the park sharing their stories. Here is the story she once shared:

Claire Douglass, son of Captain Harding Douglass, fell in love with a beautiful young woman named Bernice Mayo. The captain was tough on his son and his men, who were stationed to take over the cotton fields in Florida. While in Florida, the two lovers met along the shores of where Silver Springs sits today and immediately fell in love. The two lovers would meet in secrecy and walk the banks along the water, and Claire promised Bernice he would marry her, giving her a family heirloom bracelet. The bracelet was in place of an engagement ring until one day, he vowed he would replace it with a real ring when he could afford it.

When Captain Douglass discovered their love affair, he shipped his son off to Europe, hoping the two would forget about each other. Claire wrote to Bernice daily, but his father intercepted the letters, and Bernice confided in Aunt Silla as a healer and adviser.

One day, Bernice started to become ill and grew sicker every day. As her health worsened, and with no word from Claire, Bernice asked Aunt Silla to row her body out after her death into the springs and bury her in what would be called the Bridal Chamber. At first, Aunt Silla refused to do this, but with the threat of a curse, she eventually agreed and, upon Bernice's death, rowed her body out into the springs and gently placed her in the water, where the Bridal Chamber opened up and sucked her body in.

The following day, the day Claire had promised he would return to marry Bernice, he met with Aunt Silla, demanding to know where his bride was. Aunt Silla rowed him out to the springs where she had left Bernice's body. Immediately, he dove into the water and attempted to bring her body to the surface. When he realized he could not bring her body out from the water, he gave up, embraced the woman's body and sank to the bottom of the springs, where he could hold onto her forever.

People have reported seeing lights underneath the water where the Bridal Chamber is located, and some have even encountered a ghostly boat making its way to the exact location in the springs at night before fading away.

Another tragic love story emerging from Silver Springs is about a young man named Navarro, a member of the Tequesta tribe, who fell in love with Tululah, a beautiful lady from the Muscogee tribe. This story resembles the love story of Claire and Bernice, but as it has been told over time, there are some differences.

The Navarro tribe's chief, Satouriana, sent the young brave to the land of the Creeks to conduct a survey and report on their power over the land.

However, since the love story of Navarro and Tululah was no longer a secret, a bargain was made, and when Navarro arrived at his destination, he was captured and held prisoner for more than three months.

During his imprisonment, Tululah became heartbroken and eventually grew ill. She succumbed to her illness, and upon her request, she was buried in the deepest part of the spring, which was known as the Bridal Chamber. After her body was placed on the water's surface, it sank to the bottom, engulfed by the rocks.

Soon after her death, Navarro returned for his love and was met with the story of her death. He immediately rode out to the springs, and it seemed as if the Bridal Chamber opened up for him long enough to catch a glimpse of his would-be bride. Without hesitation, he jumped from the boat, and during their embrace, they were both swallowed up by the rocks.

Unfortunately, there is no written record of the love story between Navarro and Tululah before 1907. A reporter on loan from Talisman wrote an article for the *Ocala Evening Star* featuring this love story. It is unclear if the reporter heard the story from someone else or if she made it up herself to attract readers. Regardless of how the second love story developed, it has become a part of the park's legends and lore, shared among employees, locals and visitors.

Throughout the years, these love stories have been shared, faded away with time and reemerged with a twist to the tale. Another love story from Silver Springs is about Oklawaha, who fell in love with Winona. The two lovers were children of their tribes' chiefs and believed if their romance was discovered, it might lead to war between the two tribes.

To prevent war, the two lovers fled the area to the Chattahoochee, which is believed to be a reference to the Chattahoochee River in Georgia. Someone from one of the tribes discovered their plan and tracked them down in the woods, backing the couple onto the bluff overlooking Silver Springs. Fearing being kept apart after being caught, they held onto each other and jumped from the cliff.

Legend claims the tribes knew they made a mistake trying to keep the lovers apart, and in honor of them, they named the local spring Oklawaha in his honor and the nearby lake after her. Legend also claims the green moss that floats under the water of the lake and springs is Winona's hair.

No one knows if the love story between Oklawaha and Winona is true, but many speculate that it is a work of fiction because no one working at the park has seen historical records with this story or the names, and there are no bluffs overlooking Silver Springs.

These love stories could explain what visitors and park rangers see when walking along the banks of the waters. Several people have reported seeing apparitions standing by the waters and a ghost boat rowing out to the Bridal Chamber and hearing disembodied crying.

Continued research has led to the discovery of another love story, which leads many to believe Silver Springs was the place for lovers to meet in secrecy. Whether these stories are factual or fictional legends, they have led to many explanations behind paranormal activity within the park.

Another set of lovers emerging from the waters of Silver Springs is Mourning Dove and Running Fox, who fell in love when the area was known as Peace Camp. The couple met in this area after Running Fox, one of the best athletes, saved Mourning Dove from a poisonous snake. She immediately fell in love with him and took him back home to meet her father, who took an immediate liking to the young man.

Another man, Brown Dog, was jealous of Running Fox and angry because he had lost to Running Fox in the races. Brown Dog struck Running Fox with a stone when he saw Mourning Dove.

As he lay on the ground dying, Running Fox enchanted the area. From that time on, anyone who met and fell in love under what is known as the twisted palm would fall in love forever. Mourning Dove took her fallen lover out to the Bridal Chamber and added to the enchantment, saying if anyone took flowers from the water and walked with one in each shoe, they would find love, and anyone who put a flower from the water in one shoe would get rid of someone causing trouble in their life.

When she placed Running Fox's body in the water, it sank into the Bridal Chamber, and she followed him by wrapping a vine around a stone, which she used as an anchor around her neck as she jumped into the water.

Though these love stories have been shared throughout time, details behind each story have faded, but those who work in and visit the park can tell you the paranormal activity within the park has remained strong. Whether related to these love stories or not, paranormal activity and ghostly encounters have made Silver Springs one of the most haunted locations in the Sunshine State.

One employee shared stories about seeing and feeling a friendly ghost present in the gift shop. She believes an old maintenance mechanic causes the paranormal activity in the gift shop, and when she is alone in the shop, she hears noises as if someone or something wants her to know she is not alone.

Several employees have realized that their jobs involve encountering a ghost now and then. Many claim there is a creepy feeling in the park once the sun sets, and park rangers who live there claim something doesn't feel right. Though they cannot pinpoint what doesn't feel right, employees know there is something strange about Silver Springs.

A ghost is believed to hang out on the top floor of the ballroom, and strange things happen in the offices, such as objects moving, odd shadows and strange noises. One employee who was closing up for the night turned all the lights off, and as she went to leave, the lights turned back on and flickered. No one else was in the building with her at the time, and there were no reported electrical issues.

One night, two employees experienced something in the ballroom when cleaning and doing dishes in the back. One of the employees saw something standing near the window, illuminated by the lights from various signs outside the ballroom. She spotted a face floating in the window, looking at them from outside. The face didn't have identifiable facial features, but they knew it was a face because they recognized the floating object had ears. Nobody was there when they went to see who was outside the ballroom.

Other visitors have reported hearing strange scratching noises coming from the ladies' restroom, and when someone asks, "What is causing the scratching sound?" a bathroom stall door opens and closes. Others have reported the bathroom door opening and closing when no one else is near the door.

Some people believe the spirits haunting Silver Springs are the lovers of the legends and the spirits of Native Americans who remain behind to watch over their land. One visitor has claimed to come face to face with the spirit of a Native American in full tribal attire while in the ladies' bathroom in the ballroom. She immediately fled the area and claimed she would never return to the springs.

Whether visitors are stopping by Silver Springs for a ride on the famous glass-bottom boats, a stroll in the woods or to experience something paranormal, this Florida park has it all.

WAKULLA SPRINGS STATE PARK

WAKULLA SPRINGS

Wakulla Springs State Park has a long history and is home to the world's largest and deepest freshwater springs. Spirits linger among this ancient cypress swamp. The most popular activity at this park is the glass-bottom boat tours, where you can see the beauty of the park, learn about the park's history, catch a glimpse of native wildlife—and maybe spot one of those lingering spirits.

The beautiful sapphire waters of Wakulla Springs make this roadside attraction one of the most sought-after when traveling through Florida. The springs are home to manatees, alligators and other wildlife, and the crystal-clear waters make it possible to see these magnificent creatures in their natural habitats. The cypress swamps filling Wakulla Springs were the perfect backdrop for many old Hollywood movies and fueled the eerie sensation many feel when exploring the park.

In addition to the eerie cypress swamplands, Wakulla Springs has a long history stretching back thousands of years. Like most areas of Florida, this area was home to early Native Americans who established small shoreline villages. It is also believed that mastodons once roamed the area, now home to alligators, manatees and an abundance of birds.

There is no doubt that Wakulla Springs is a creepy place, and the knowledge of paranormal events in the park's history enhances the eeriness. Many of the park's ghostly encounters occur in the Wakulla Springs Lodge, where many guests have complained to the front desk. When in

A limpkin at Wakulla Springs. *State Archives of Florida.*

a guest room, several people have heard sounds of a loud party in the adjacent room, including voices and clinking glasses. Upon complaining to the front desk, guests learn there is no one in the room where the sounds are coming from.

This 1930s hacienda-style lodge is suitable for those visiting Wakulla Springs hoping to come face to face with something supernatural. The hotel was built on the swamplands in southern Florida to preserve the area's natural environment; it has also preserved a location for spirits to hang out.

Other paranormal reports in the lodge include guests feeling like someone is touching their feet and sometimes pulling on them when sleeping. Room 23 seems to be the most active room, where guests have seen apparitions, heard strange noises and had their personal belongings disappear to reappear later in the day in a different location from where they left them.

With such a long history, there is no doubt Wakulla Springs is the perfect place to experience paranormal activity. Whether it is the spirits of Native Americans, past visitors or owners of the land who haunt the land, something eerie lurks in the shadows among the primeval cypress swamps.

POTTER'S WAX MUSEUM

ST. AUGUSTINE

Potter's Wax Museum is a classic, old-school wax museum. At one point in St. Augustine's history, it was the second-largest wax museum in the world and the first in the United States. This museum features a unique assembly of historical figures and celebrities frozen in time.

Visitors step back in time as they enter through an old apothecary into one of the most haunted places in St. Augustine. Once inside, visitors face the courage, greatness, innovation and incredible talents of those who helped shape our country and the world into what they are today. These innovators shaped our culture like the creators of the wax museum did when sculpting the displays in Potter's Wax Museum.

Since 1949, Potter's Wax Museum has been a popular destination for tourists and locals looking for a unique place to visit and explore St. Augustine. The founder, George Potter, had a vision and watched it come to life until he passed in 1979. After his death, his family managed the building before selling off most of the museum's collection.

As much of Potter's beloved collection was being sold off one by one, Dottie White, a former curator for the museum, bought the remaining wax figures. She reopened the legendary wax museum in 1987, renaming it Potter's House of Wax. Then, in 2013, the museum moved into the Oldest Drug Store, which remains on Orange Street today.

There are very few reports about paranormal activity occurring in the museum, but several people have experienced an eerie feeling when visiting the museum. Some have felt like they are being watched, while

Top: Potter's Wax Museum, St. Augustine. *Karl E. Holland, State Archives of Florida.*

Middle: A barbarian warrior on display at Potter's Wax Museum. *James L. Gaines, State Archives of Florida.*

Bottom: A costumed young woman poses with a Roman warrior displayed at Potter's Wax Museum. *Ted Newhall, State Archives of Florida.*

others believe they have spotted shadow figures darting among the wax figures, and when they look closer, no one is there. Could the spirits hanging around Potter's Wax Museum be the ghosts of former visitors, employees or Potter himself? Or could it be possible that spirits are haunting the locations that are attached to the historic and antique items, such as props and clothing used in the museum? There is also the possibility that the place had spirits roaming long before the wax museum moved in, and those spirits decided to stay.

Regardless of what haunts Potter's Wax Museum, it is an eerie place to visit—day or night.

GREENWOOD CEMETERY

ORLANDO

The City of Orlando did not offer residents a permanent burial location until the 1880s. The lack of a proper cemetery led to many graves becoming lost, especially when new homes and businesses were built during the city's boom.

Newspaper publisher Mahlon Gore led a campaign with eight Orlando residents who pulled together to purchase twenty-six acres of land from John W. Anderson for $1,800.[5] The land was transformed into Greenwood Cemetery, and Samuel A. Robinson designed the original layout. The City of Orlando owns and operates Greenwood Cemetery, which has become a significant part of the city's history and one of the most visited haunted locations in Central Florida.

Greenwood Cemetery is the final resting place for many Orlando-area residents, including some better-known residents, such as T.G. Lee, Mayor Bob Carr, Mayor Mahlon Gore, Joe Tinker and Joseph Bumby. Thomas Jefferson's grandson Francis Wayles Eppes (1801–1881) is buried in Greenwood Cemetery.

Though cemeteries are not always haunted by those who are buried there, Greenwood Cemetery is one of the most haunted locations in Central Florida. Paranormal reports include visitors seeing floating apparitions; hearing disembodied voices, laughter and melodies; and encountering strange, unexplainable smells.

So, who haunts Greenwood Cemetery? One theory is that the spirit of Fred Weeks, a northern businessman, remains behind to haunt the land he moved to Florida to purchase. Upon realizing the area was nothing but swampland, Weeks realized he had been ripped off by the three English attorneys who sold him the land. Unable to get his money back, Weeks bought a plot of land at the entrance to the cemetery, where he erected a tombstone with the three attorneys' names. The tombstone was inscribed with a biblical verse from Luke 10:30: "A certain man went down from Jerusalem to Jericho and fell among thieves." Weeks wanted everyone to know he had been duped and by whom.

Later, the three attorneys repurchased the land, including the area at Greenwood Cemetery's entrance, and demolished the tombstone bearing their names. But that did not stop Weeks from getting his revenge. He later bought another plot of land about one hundred feet away from the original tombstone. On this plot of land within the cemetery, he inscribed the same verse from Luke 10:30 on a mausoleum, which also had an area that would have been large enough to fit the three attorneys' names. However, the names were not there, and some believe the families of the three men chiseled them off. This mausoleum is the final resting place of Weeks, who is believed to have died alone after his wife took their children and left.

Many believe that Weeks is still furious over being scammed, and even in death, he refuses to give up seeking revenge. Many people have seen the spirit of Weeks standing in front of his mausoleum.

In addition to the disgruntled spirit of Fred Weeks, there is a creepy section of the Greenwood Cemetery known as Babyland. This area of the cemetery is set aside as the final resting place for children under the age of five. Many of the children buried in Babyland died at the Sunland Hospital, which was where tuberculosis patients were treated, and the facility was later used as a behavioral center for mentally challenged youth. A high percentage of patients were still infants when treated at Sunland Hospital, with many dying on the same day they were born. Several tombstones in Babyland don't have the child's name engraved and are inscribed with a single date— their birth and death date.

When exploring Babyland, especially sections one and three, visitors report hearing sounds of children laughing and playing and the soft melodic sounds of a child's music box. Other paranormal reports in this area of Greenwood Cemetery include feeling strange sensations, tugging of their pants and other interactions as if a child is trying to gain the attention of those who visit. Though rare, there are some reports of people seeing ghostly figures the size of children running around and playing among the tombstones of Greenwood Cemetery, especially near Babyland.

Set on the highest point of Greenwood Cemetery is the Wilmott Mausoleum, belonging to an influential Orlando family. The Wilmott family was in real estate in the early nineteenth century, and though they were a powerful family in the community, they were not without tragedy. Their grandson, Fred Wilmott Jr., and Frank Pounds Jr. (a family friend) were at a swimming hole together at the age of five. The two misjudged the depth of the water and waded in too deep. The two boys drowned, and Fred and members of his family are buried in the mausoleum. Cemetery visitors have reported seeing apparitions appearing at the Wilmott Mausoleum. The most commonly reported spirit seen near the mausoleum is a man dressed in an old-fashioned military uniform. It seems the soldier is looking off into the distance, and it is unknown if this spirit is related to the Wilmott family.

Greenwood Cemetery is also the final resting place for many veterans from all of the past wars. The cemetery has a special military section for World War I, World War II, Spanish-American War, Korean War and Vietnam War veterans. Many visitors have reported seeing apparitions dressed in military clothing wandering the cemetery. These spirits tend to fade away and vanish upon being noticed.

As the oldest and largest cemetery in Orlando, Greenwood Cemetery does not disappoint. This is the perfect place for historians to learn more about the city's history and for paranormal enthusiasts to encounter something supernatural.

GRAVE OF AMERICA'S OLDEST MAN

BARTOW

According to the *1981 Guinness Book of World Records*,[6] America's oldest man is a man named Charlie Smith. Charlie was born in West Africa on July 4, 1842, and he lived in Florida until he died on October 5, 1979. Living 137 years, Charlie witnessed many things, including more than twenty-five U.S. presidents, the first moon landing, many technological inventions and much more.[7]

After his death, Charlie was buried in Polk County, Florida, in the small town of Bartow. Today, his grave is one of America's most popular and oddly intriguing roadside attractions. Visitors worldwide come to Polk County for an opportunity to see where the oldest man in America was buried.

So, who was Charlie Smith? Originally named Mitchell Watkins, Charlie was taken from his Liberia home and brought to the United States. Upon his arrival, he was sold into slavery to a rancher, Charlie Smith. Upon the rancher's death, Charlie took his owner's name. In his twenties, Charlie became a free man after the signing of the Emancipation Proclamation.

Charlie lived a full life, doing many different things, including being a part of the Union army, an expert gambler, a bounty hunter with the Jesse James Gang, a circus member, a father and a husband. He believed his vitamins, taken with a shot of rum, kept him healthy despite his various health conditions.

Upon his death, Bartow residents contributed to a fund to pay for a tombstone engraved with "America's Oldest Man." Charlie is buried in Woodland Cemetery in row 28.

This page: The Grave of the Oldest Man in America, Charlie Smith, who lived 137 years, is located in Bartow. *By Heather Leigh, PhD.*

BRADEN CASTLE RUINS

BRADENTON

In the mid-1800s, living in Florida was challenging, as many families faced settling in a new area known for hostilities between newcomers and Natives. Dr. Joseph Braden came to the area wanting to build a home on the river that was secure and hostile-Native proof. In 1851, he made what is known today as the Braden Castle, and though it was solid and believed to be attack-proof, it was attacked by Natives in 1856.

During the night attack, Dr. Braden and his guests stood their ground upstairs, firing on the hostiles. During their retreat, the Natives ran into the woods, taking several enslaved people, blankets and mules with them. The following day, the men from the castle tracked down the Natives on an island in the middle of a creek. During an hour-long battle, three Native Americans were shot, and the sub-chief of the Billy Bowlegs band and several others managed to escape.

It was a sad day when Dr. Braden lost his castle during the panic of 1857, leaving the property in the hands of his major creditor. Then, in 1903, the castle caught fire, which gutted the entire structure, and it has been crumbling and in ruins ever since. After that, the property changed hands several times until it fell into the hands of the Camping Tourists of America.

Tin can tourists started traveling to Florida, checking out various roadside attractions, including many arriving in Florida around 1919 in their Ford Model Ts. Florida was the place for northerners to escape cold winters and enjoy time exploring the Sunshine State. As part of the Camping Tourists of America, people would come to the property where the Braden Castle is located to enjoy camping around the skeletal remains of the castle.

Braden Castle, Bradenton. *State Archives of Florida.*

The Braden Castle Ruins is in Braden Castle Park and is listed on the National Register of Historic Places. The park showcases the exciting history of local pioneers, the castle and the area's historical significance. Many who have visited Braden Castle have encountered paranormal entities and reported multiple ghostly encounters. Could it be the dilapidated property that nature has reclaimed that creates an eerie feeling? Or could it be the spirits of Dr. Braden and others who remain behind to haunt the ruins of the castle? Anything is possible, and several people have witnessed paranormal activity throughout the ruins.

The screams of those who died on the property during the Third Seminole War can be heard echoing through the woods, and several trespassers have reported being terrorized by an unknown apparition. Campers have heard strange sounds from behind the remaining castle walls and sounds of footsteps that seem to be circling campers in an attempt to scare them off.

One legend has two brave explorers following the sounds of footsteps with handmade torches to discover no one else at the ruins with them. They were heading back to their camp when a ghost jumped out of the darkness and lunged at them, grabbing one of the men and pulling him toward an unknown darkness. After recovering from the attack, the two continued exploring the area until they came face to face with a fierce creature, which they believed was the same creature that had been torturing campers for more than half a decade.

It is unknown if this story is true or just a legend, but it has campers sharing the story around the campfire, scaring young children from going off into the wooded areas. Whether this story is true or just a legend, there is no doubt that the Braden Castle ruins are haunted. Just ask anyone who has camped or visited the area.

Johnnie Brown's Grave—The Human Monkey

Palm Beach

Hidden among the ferns of the Pizza Al Fresco courtyard is a unique cemetery containing many secrets. Though this cemetery, the only one in Palm Beach proper, is technically a pet cemetery, it is the final resting place for a spider monkey that was more than a pet to Addison Mizner.

Mizner was a jazz era architect whose vibrant Mediterranean Revival designs remain part of the signature styles of many Palm Beach–area resorts. Mizner's spider monkey, Johnnie Brown "the Human Monkey," was one of his many exotic and unusual pets. The monkey accompanied Mizner to all of his high-society events. Johnnie Brown had several brushes with politics, including the Scopes Trial, where a teacher was on trial for teaching evolution to his students. The spider monkey also ran for mayor and was backed and supported by his owner for this endeavor.

After Mizner died in 1927, the town permitted his beloved pets to be buried outside his Villa Mizner mansion. Johnnie was buried in the courtyard next to Scottish terrier Laddie, owned by a neighbor.

Architect Addison Mizner.
State Archives of Florida.

The famous spider monkey and his canine graveyard companion, Laddie, are both laid to rest in the Pizza Al Fresco courtyard. The two have been spotted playfully haunting the plaza and nearby boutiques along Worth Avenue in Palm Beach. Many have seen the two chasing each other through the courtyard and wrestling in the flower beds. When the two spirits are noticed, they scamper into Mizner's mansion.

Several local business owners instruct employees to leave monkey dishes (small ramekins) of sliced bananas out at night for the playful pair.

Johnnie's and Laddie's gravestones are nestled on the southern side of the Pizza Al Fresco courtyard. They are typically surrounded by tables of four on either side of the two gravestones.

MYSTERY OF THE WITCH'S WALL

PALM BEACH

The north end of the island of Palm Beach hides a mysterious secret that has been the source of urban legends passed down through generations. Along Country Club Road is a stretch of coral rock, the source of the mysterious legends. This area has become known as the Witch's Wall.

One legend shared among generations of locals is of an evil witch who lived on the island. This witch kidnaps children, trapping them inside her coral cave, and the only way to free one of her captives is to touch the wall. Once the trapped soul is released from the wall, the witch will go on a mission to find another soul to trap.

Others have reported hearing moans of a mourning mother coming from nearby, which could be connected to a woman who had lost her husband. She lived in the area, and one night after her son moved out, she asked him to visit for Thanksgiving. On his way over with his family, the car crashed, killing everyone in the vehicle. The area where the accident occurred is believed to be the haunted section of the road near the Witch's Wall. Many say the woman's cries and moans are her grieving her lost family.

Adding to the mystery behind the Witch's Wall is a small barred window on the south side of the coral rock wall. Several passersby have reported seeing an eerie glow from this window at night. However, it has been proven that the glow comes from a nearby streetlight casting its shadow across the coral formation and through the bars.

Another intriguing story behind the Witch's Wall is of a wealthy man who kept his crazy mother hidden away. He trapped her in a dungeon believed to be behind the mysterious bars. Every once in a while, passersby would see her if they stopped and peeked inside the window. This story has been shared so often that when people stop by and peer in the window, they believe they can see a woman trapped in it. Unfortunately, for those seeking a ghostly story to share, it is not the spirit of a woman they see but a water pump for the water pumping station in West Palm Beach.

ORANGE COUNTY REGIONAL HISTORICAL CENTER

ORLANDO

Central Florida has ties to one of the most notorious and ingenious serial killers of all time. Ted Bundy was tried for the murder of Kimberly Leach in 1980 at the Orlando courthouse. The location of his trial is now the location of the Orange County Regional Historical Center. During his trial, Bundy reportedly carved his name into the table he was sitting at.

Many people believe the building is haunted by the spirit of Bundy, who continues to wreak havoc on the living. His spirit is tied to the levitation of objects and many strange occurrences in the building. In addition to seeing Bundy's spirit, several eyewitnesses have reported seeing ghostly lawyers where courtrooms were located.

Other ghostly encounters and experiences at the historic center include office workers hearing the sounds of a party, glasses clinking and loud laughter. Some have also fallen victim to being locked in a room after the doors mysteriously locked on their own.

Whoever or whatever is haunting the Orange County Regional Historical Center is making their existence known.

SMALLWOOD TRADING POST

CHOKOLOSKEE

The Smallwood Trading Post was popular in Chokoloskee and has remained unchanged since 1982. This trading post is like an actual step back in time, which could be one of the many reasons it is one of the most haunted locations in Florida.

Ted Smallwood opened the Smallwood Trading Post in 1906 to provide the community with a general store and trading post. The original concept of the store was to serve the community, and today, it serves the dead. The small trading post is now a time capsule for the community, serving as a museum where travelers can stop and enjoy a break from their road trip.

Rumors in the small community of Chokoloskee connect the area to the notorious outlaw Edgar Watson, who had a horrendous temper and a penchant for murder. It is unknown how many victims he had, but people in the town whispered about him killing workers in the sugar cane fields so he wouldn't have to pay them for their products or services.

Today, locals claim the paranormal activity in town is related to the needs of Watson's victims seeking revenge. It is believed these souls followed Watson, tracking him to Chokoloskee, where they tormented him. These souls troubled Watson until he tried to get their forgiveness by doing one good deed.

His one good deed may have been too little too late, but he gave it all he had. In 1910, a woman was killed in Watson's home, and he made it his mission to seek revenge and kill the man responsible for her death. Watson went to the trading post to purchase bullets and started raving about his

Smallwood's store, Chokoloskee. *State Archives of Florida.*

plans to kill another man. Though he was seeking revenge, the townsfolk were tired of his emotionless acts of violence and took matters into their own hands. An angry mob of locals cornered Watson inside the trading post and gunned him down. Locals believe his spirit is now trapped inside the Smallwood Trading Post.

Poor Edgar Watson is now stuck in his version of hell. Many people have seen his apparition inside the Smallwood Trading Post. His body is riddled with bullets, and his face seems to be in a frozen state, as if he is screaming in pain.

In addition to Watson's spirit haunting this small trading post, there are rumors in town about the spirit of the woman he was said to be seeking revenge for. Many residents believe that if Watson succeeded in buying ammunition, tracking down her killer and finally getting the revenge she needed, her spirit would be able to rest in peace. However, since Watson was gunned down before this could happen, her spirit is believed to roam the area in search of her revenge.

Several patrons of the Smallwood Trading Post claim that they see her spirit more than his, but she is barely recognizable as a human when she is spotted. Her body rotates, and her skin and flesh hang loosely off her skeleton.

This woman's spirit is often seen in front of the bedroom dresser mirror. She appears to be attempting to comb what is left of her hair. While combing her hair, she begins to cry and eventually fades away. Visitors can see her reflection in the mirror when standing before the dresser. Some visitors describe the experience as if they have come face to face with a real-life zombie. Upon being startled, these visitors turn around to see who is behind them and discover they are alone in the room.

Has this woman turned into a zombie in the afterlife? Or is she a wraith? Or is it possible she is a deformed ghost lost between worlds? Whichever option it is, everyone claims to feel a great sense of fear when seeing her spirit in the trading post.

BROWNIE THE POST OFFICE DOG

DAYTONA BEACH

It was a sad Halloween when Daytona Beach's Brownie died in 1954. However, many who knew the beloved dog that won residents' love and was named the Town Dog of Daytona Beach believed Brownie still explored, played and interacted with residents.

So, who is Brownie? Let's look at this dog's life and how he became Daytona Beach's town dog.

One day in 1940, Brownie showed up in downtown Daytona Beach. When he arrived on Beach Street, this dog was about one year old. Brownie liked to hang out at the Daytona Cab Company. The owner, Ed Budgen, and his cab drivers constructed a doghouse for Brownie and set up a bank account in the dog's name at Florida Bank and Trust. (Today, the account is at the same bank under the name of Halifax Historical Society Museum, and you can make donations through the bank.) Locals helped fund Brownie's bank account from donations from residents, community merchants and tourists. All money raised by the community was used to help pay for Brownie's veterinary care, food, housing and other needs.

The community pulled together to purchase Brownie's annual dog license. His tag was always #1. This represented that he was the goodwill ambassador for Daytona Beach. Local merchants provided Brownie with plenty of food, especially steak and ice cream. It was well known Brownie loved ice cream, and he could eat an entire pint in one sitting.

Brownie became so popular that when shoppers and tourists came to Beach Street, they would stop, greet him and take photos with him. It was not uncommon for visitors to sit with him while waiting for a bus or cab. If Brownie were missing or limping, people would ask, "Is Brownie okay?"

Word about Brownie spread, and he appeared in national magazines and newspapers. His daily antics were covered regularly by reporters from local Daytona Beach newspapers. Brownie would receive Christmas cards and presents from residents and people worldwide every year.

Sadly, Brownie died on Halloween in 1954. At the age of fifteen, he was struggling with a long illness. His funeral and obituary were featured on the front page of the *Daytona Beach News-Journal*—twice.

At the time of Brownie's death, it was against the law (and still is today) to bury anything in the local park. However, Mayor Jack Tamm changed the laws for a single day, allowing Brownie to be buried on the corner of Beach Street and Orange Avenue. This location is directly across the street from where his doghouse stood and clearly views the Daytona Cab Company.

In addition to the seventy-five people who attended Brownie's funeral, several stray dogs, including his fellow stray dog friend Stinky, participated in the funeral. Mayor Tamm gave Brownie's eulogy during the funeral on November 2, 1954, reminding everyone that Brownie was "a good dog." Brownie's pallbearers were several prominent businessmen and city officials, and the words "A Good Dog" were etched on his tombstone.

Many years later, a second Brownie came to town, becoming the post office mascot. The new Brownie appeared at the Beach Street Post Office, and since he hung around the area, he was named the post office mascot, considered an official employee of the post office.

Like the previous Brownie, this Brownie also had his own bank account. He lived from 1955 until 1970; visitors can see his grave next to the post office. The second Brownie was not as famous as his predecessor, but many in the Daytona Beach community loved and cared for him.

The second Brownie's grave was visited daily by tourists and locals until it disappeared in the late 1980s. Luckily, in 1994, the grave was rediscovered, and the spirit of Brownie continues to be celebrated.

One ghostly story about Brownie is about when Brownie's Dog Boutique opened in Daytona. A few weeks after the store opened, a homeless man entered the shop declaring, "I just saw Brownie get hit by a car!" The owner told him Brownie had died in 1954, so this was very unlikely. It is unknown if the homeless man was hallucinating or if he was seeing the spirit of Brownie running in the street and getting hit by a car.

Another interesting story comes from the same store. The store owners were hosting a party when a woman came to the party by herself. The woman hung out all night alone, never interacting with the other guests. The following day, the same strange woman came into the store. The woman told the shopkeepers her mother had recently passed, and she hadn't entered her mother's room since. She came to the party the night before because her mom loved playing with Brownie and had shared many stories about the dog with her. After the party, the woman finally went into her mother's room, where she looked at a book her mother had been reading when she died. Inside the book was the article about Brownie's death in 1954. She couldn't believe the coincidence and claimed she felt drawn to attend the party in honor of her mother and Brownie.

It is safe to say that when alive, Brownie positively impacted the community and continues to impact many people in death.

Dr. Mudd at Fort Jefferson

Dry Tortugas National Park

Fort Jefferson has a unique feel about it. From the moment you arrive on the island in the Dry Tortugas, you can feel the energy of this location. Many have also claimed that the island has a heavy presence, and some feel spooked and never return to the fort. But the eerie feelings and hauntingly scary stories have not stopped people from adding the Dry Tortugas National Park to their road trip itinerary.

With such a tragic past, Fort Jefferson can be haunted by the spirits of soldiers, pirates, prisoners and the many others who came to the island but experienced nothing but disaster and tragedy. Many believe one of the spirits haunting Fort Jefferson is Dr. Samuel Alexander Mudd, who was imprisoned at Fort Jefferson for his role in the assassination of President Abraham Lincoln.

Dr. Mudd was Fort Jefferson's most famous prisoner, leaving his historical mark and psychic energy imprint on the island. He was born on December 20, 1833, in Maryland, approximately thirty miles from Washington, D.C. He started practicing medicine in 1856 upon graduating from Baltimore Medical College (the University of Maryland). He happily lived life practicing medicine and farming. Dr. Mudd married Sarah Frances Dyer, and they had nine children together.

Dr. Mudd was arrested on April 26, 1865, for his part in the conspiracy to assassinate President Lincoln. He was sentenced to life in prison on June 29, 1865, and was sent to serve his sentence at Fort Jefferson. He and three of his convicted co-conspirators—Edmund Spangler, Samuel Arnold and Michael O'Laughlen—arrived at Fort Jefferson.

This page: Fort Jefferson, Garden Key, Key West. *Joseph Trotten, Library of Congress.*

Throughout the years, Dr. Mudd attempted to escape, and one of his most talked-about escape attempts was when he tried to hide on a supply ship. Though his attempts to escape failed, Dr. Mudd was eventually released for the role he played when yellow fever swept through the prison and fort. His wife continually wrote letters to President Andrew Johnson to have her beloved husband released from jail.

Dr. Mudd was assigned to the prison's carpentry shop until, one day, he leaped into action, returning to his medical duties. Some claim his role in treating patients, prisoners and soldiers during the yellow fever epidemic at

Fort Jefferson, officers' quarters. *Joseph Trotten, Library of Congress.*

Fort Jefferson was heroic. In 1867, he helped diagnose and treat those who contracted yellow fever. He treated those at the prison from August 18 to November 14, 1867.

In recognition of his efforts, President Johnson signed Dr. Mudd's pardon in front of Mudd's wife. His pardon was signed on February 8, 1869, and then Dr. Mudd was officially released from the confines of Fort Jefferson's jail on March 8, 1869. Arnold and Spangler were also pardoned by President Andrew Johnson and released from prison for assisting as nurses during the yellow fever outbreak.

Though he left the Dry Tortugas after his pardon, Dr. Mudd definitely left his mark on the island through his bravery and swift action during the epidemic. He died on January 10, 1883, at forty-nine, after battling pneumonia.

Many visitors to Fort Jefferson head straight to Dr. Mudd's cell, which is on the fort's bottom level, past the Park Headquarters. Many people have experienced strange, unexplainable occurrences when in the cell. Some people have witnessed shadow figures from the prison cell and strange light anomalies. Other paranormal activities claimed to occur near Dr. Mudd's cell include hearing the slamming of cell doors, disembodied voices, footsteps and men crying.

In addition to Dr. Mudd's spirit haunting Fort Jefferson, the area is a ghostly hotbed sitting off the coast of Florida in the warm waters of the Gulf of Mexico. The island in the Dry Tortugas has a horrific past, including cannibalism, murder, executions, drownings, shipwrecks and more. Like many of the hurricanes that have swept through the Dry Tortugas, Fort Jefferson is the perfect storm of paranormal activity.

The Dry Tortugas National Park is riddled with paranormal occurrences, including encounters with poltergeists and specters. Many park rangers who have patrolled the fort at night come back with chilling stories to share with other rangers and their families.

Paranormal activity throughout Fort Jefferson includes eerie feelings, unusual energies, strange lights and devilish sounds around midnight. Overnight camping is allowed on the island, and those who have braved spending the night have claimed to be woken up at night to screams; when going out to investigate the source of the screams, they come face to face with scary shadow people who dart around the island.

Visitors have reported seeing similar shadow figures within the walls of the fort. In addition to shadowing people, it is rumored the Hatman has made his appearance known now and then.

How are the spirits coming and going from Fort Jefferson? Some believe there is a vortex or portal near the jail cells. This portal is also rumored to be captured in photos, appearing as a swirling mass of light and dark winding around one another in the center of the jail cell halls.

Ten-Mile Brick Road—Old Brick Highway

Espanola

Nestled in Flagler County and southern St. Johns County is a quiet scrub forest. Within this scrub forest hides a red brick road, once a famous thoroughfare hosting a regular stream of tin can tourists. As travelers made their way to Florida in their Model T Fords, pulling silver, shimmering mobile homes, new roads developed, providing easy access for travelers from as far as Chicago to the exotic, tropical wilderness Florida offers.

As more and more people traveled to Florida, new highways and freeways speckled Florida's landscape, making travel faster and more accessible. When more efficient roads opened, the tiny red brick road in Espanola became a thing of the past. The portion of the road in Espanola was originally named Dixie Highway and eventually became obsolete in 1916.

Once travelers stopped using this road, it allowed Mother Nature to take control back and the spirits of the area to roam free. However, there is a ten-mile stretch remaining, but much of this area is riddled with potholes and covered in sand. Additionally, many of the bricks from Old Dixie Highway were used to build the gymnasium for the Bunnell Elementary School.

The run-down brick highway is only nine feet wide, leaving barely enough room for one car to drive it. Luckily, this forgotten stretch of Florida highway does not greet much modern-day traffic.

Those who have braved traveling down the Old Brick Highway in Espanola are often lucky enough to capture a glimpse of the supernatural entities known to remain in the area. The most common report of paranormal activity is seeing bright balls of light, about the size of a basketball, off in the distance, dashing in and out from behind trees of the wooded area. Upon closer investigation, the ball of light either vanishes into thin air or, it has been reported, shoots straight up into the sky.

Other paranormal reports include hearing cries and screams emanating from the woods. Many believe these sounds are from a banshee who hides in the woods waiting for her next victim.

The most interesting paranormal reports are the sightings and interactions of a lifelike apparition. Many people have reported talking with an older gentleman while exploring the area near the road, and as they parted ways, they turned back to look at him, and he vanished. No one knows who this gentleman is or why he haunts this stretch of the Old Dixie Highway in Espanola.

FAILED HOLLOW EARTH UTOPIA

ESTERO

Koreshan State Park is where it was once believed utopia was located in Estero, Florida. For a brief time, it was thought that Estero was where a utopian branch of Christianity settled, calling the area the New Jerusalem. The group settled in the area in 1894 but faded away in the 1930s.

Though many believed Cyrus Teed, the founder of the Koreshan Unity movement, was a nut, several followers believed in his vision and followed him to Florida. In Florida, Teed and his several hundred followers created the perfect community, where everyone worked together to create the ultimate utopia here on Earth. The community was named the Koreshan Unity after Teed renamed himself Koresh.

So, who was this man so many people followed to the farthest southern reaches of the United States in search of the perfect world? Let's look closer at Teed and the community he built here in Florida.

Teed believed we were already living on the inside of Earth, and with suitable instruments, we could see around the world into any country we desired. He thought the theory behind gravity was a lie and that centrifugal force was holding people to the Earth. So, if gravity was a lie, what did Teed believe the sun to be? Teed's theory about the sun was that batteries powered it.

Teed also believed that with a strong enough telescope you could see other parts of the world. For example, from Florida you could see what was happening on the streets of London using this telescope. Hitler later embraced the idea behind this theory and put many scientists to work to create the perfect telescope to allow him to spy on other countries from the comfort of his home.

Teed died on December 22, 1908, and his disciples refused to have him buried. They believed he would rise from the dead as Teed had predicted. As his followers waited for his resurrection, they placed Teed's body in a bathtub for several days. When he didn't

Aerial view looking north over the Koreshan State Historic Site park in Estero. *State Archives of Florida.*

rise from the dead, the group was ordered by local officials to bury his body.

Teed's body was laid to rest in a tomb on the southern tip of Estero Island, where his followers held twenty-four-hour vigils to monitor the tomb for when he came back to life. Unfortunately, there were no signs of resurrection, and during the 1921 hurricane, Teed's mausoleum and body were washed out to sea.

The last four Koreshan survivors deeded their utopia to the State of Florida in 1961. Only a few buildings remain and are part of the state park, where visitors can see Teed's rectilineator, the model he made of the inside-out world he wholeheartedly believed in.

Today, ghosts of the Koreshan Unity roam the grounds, reliving the life they once believed was utopia here on Earth. Several people have reported hearing voices while exploring the remaining structures and seeing full-bodied apparitions wandering the grounds of the former cult. Many people have claimed to have seen Teed standing off to the side, almost as if he is watching over his prized project.

Could the paranormal activity be related to the members of the Koreshan Unity movement? Some believe the spirits from the group remain behind to protect their beliefs and continue to live their utopian life.

VALUJET FLIGHT 592 CRASH MEMORIAL

EVERGLADES

ValuJet flight 592 crashed into the Everglades in May 1996, and many people have witnessed multiple paranormal events in the area near the memorial. The crash killed all 110 people on board, and a memorial site and marker were erected in honor of those who lost their lives.

One hauntingly creepy story was told by a Miccosukee Native American girl who spoke to others about seeing the spirits of the dead from flight 592 rising and wandering throughout the crash site. As the story continues to be shared, it is almost described as a scene from *The Walking Dead*. This is similar to the reports of spirits rising from land around the 9/11 Ground Zero Memorial in New York City.

Other people have seen apparitions on the road along the Tamiami Trail, including a man standing on the side of the road grinning and another man trying to wave the driver down to stop and help. Most drivers are afraid to stop and keep driving without making eye contact. Many of those who have ignored the spirits on the side of the road have claimed to have an apparition suddenly appear in the passenger's seat of their vehicle or feel the heavy presence of them no longer being alone in the car.

Those who have stopped get out of the car to realize there is no one in the area, and they are all alone. If someone had been in the area, the driver would have seen them running or hiding, as this area is flatland and nothing is around.

Devil's Millhopper Geological State Park

Gainesville

Gainesville, Florida, is a college town where adventure awaits around every corner. Though most of the community centers on the University of Florida—"Go Gators!"—its location provides explorers many opportunities to be outdoors, where they can become one with nature. The best thing about Gainesville is that it allows for educational opportunities and experiences for everyone, including paranormal enthusiasts.

Devil's Millhopper Geological State Park is a paranormal gem hidden among the hustle and bustle of attending school in Gainesville. The state park is home to a massive natural sinkhole measuring 120 feet deep and 500 feet wide. The name "Devil's Millhopper" comes from the bones and fossils at the bottom of the sinkhole, resembling a millhopper funnel. It was believed the devil used this sinkhole and it was where he fed on the bodies of the living and then hid their bones at the bottom.

Though Devil's Millhopper Geological State Park is famous among naturalists and geologists, the park holds a dark secret. Though many believed the devil used the sinkhole, legend claims he made himself home in the Gainesville area many moons ago, when he fell in love with a local Indian woman. Because she did not love him back, he kidnapped her, running deep into the forest. As the devil ran away with the woman, braves followed in pursuit to rescue her. When he realized he had nowhere else to run, the devil stopped, breaking open the Earth. As the enormous hole opened, he jumped in to escape, and as they disappeared into the sinkhole, he turned the braves into stone. Knowing this legend, paranormal explorers worldwide make their way to Devil's Millhopper Geological State Park to conduct experiments and attempt to communicate with the devil.

One of the most active areas of the park is near the waterfall. Many people who approach the waterfall feel a sense of dread and experience intense emotions and drastic temperature changes. It has been said that the temperature changes feel like walking from the hot, humid Florida heat directly into a walk-in freezer.

Some people who have visited the waterfall at the state park have had the urge to run away from the area, especially after looking into the falls and seeing a humanoid creature with glowing eyes staring back at them. A variation of the story is that the humanoid creature is a matte gray color and the eyes are much larger than human eyes and pitch black.

Other paranormal activities experienced at the state park include hearing a woman screaming and strange moaning and seeing shadow figures darting around among the trees. It is also reported that paranormal activity at Devil's Millhopper Geological State Park picks up when there is a full moon.

1894 Old County Jail

Green Cove Springs

Set in Green Cove Springs is the 1894 Old County Jail, which housed several violent criminals, including one convicted axe murderer. Not only did this sixteen-cell jail provide a place to hold criminals, but today, it continues to house many spirits who remain behind, haunting the location.

The Old County Jail was known for housing the worst of the worst among criminals; it was also where capital punishment was carried out. Up until 1915, this jail was where criminals sentenced to death were sent and hanged on the gallows, which remain on the property today. The 1894 Old County Jail in Green Cove Springs was closed as a place of incarceration in 1972.

Today, the town archivist's office is in the Old County Jail, where much of the town's historic information and artifacts are housed. On display at the jail are old crime guns and a creepy dummy wearing prison stripes hanging out of one of the barred windows by his fingertips.

The archivist on duty is no stranger to the ghosts from the past who call the Old County Jail home. Paranormal investigators have been invited into the Old Jail, where they have captured dozens of EVPs, including voices of spirits telling them to "Get out!" There are so many unique EVPs from this location that the archivist has dozens of files saved on her computer to preserve the paranormal activity at the 1894 Old County Jail.

Eerie EVPs are not the only thing experienced when visiting and investigating the Old County Jail. In addition to the building looking creepy, people visiting the structure have experienced disembodied voices, strange creaking noises, doors opening and closing and hair pulling.

With so much activity happening in all areas of the Old Jail, there is a high probability it is haunted by former inmates who continue with their jailbird antics.

Shoreline Park—The UFO Mecca

Gulf Breeze

When you hear UFO stories, most come from the desert region of the United States, such as Area 51. Not many people know about the series of UFO sightings that have occurred in Florida, known as the Gulf Breeze UFO Incident.

On November 11, 1987, a local contractor, Ed Walters, captured images he claimed to be a UFO over the Gulf Breeze area. These images were published in the *Gulf Breeze Sentinel* newspaper. Walters claimed to suddenly become immobilized by a blue beam of light, and when he was freed, he managed to take five Polaroids from the sky. The pictures revealed that above his home, there was an object hovering approximately two hundred feet above the ground. This event was described as "right out of a Spielberg movie." He claimed to have been visited multiple times by the same mysterious flying vessel for several months. During this time, he recorded video and took thirty-two photographs of the object.

The images were analyzed by experts, such as UFOlogist Bruce Maccabee, who believed the photographs were authentic. However, as with most paranormal activity captured in video and still photos, many others in the field suspected the images to be part of an elaborate hoax.

Walters later claimed he also witnessed the same craft land on Soundside Drive, where it deposited five aliens on the road. According to his eyewitness report, one of these aliens looked into a window of his home and spoke to him telepathically in English and Spanish. During their conversation, the aliens gave him a book with images of dogs.

During his December 2, 1987 visit, he reported being immobilized again by the blue beam, which lifted him three feet off the ground. Then, several months later, he allegedly photographed his wife fleeing from the same blue beam. These incidents were some of the nineteen total sightings and encounters Walters and his family had over time. The series of UFO sightings in the area continued through May 1, 1988.

During these UFO encounters and experiences, Walters also claimed to have suffered from missing time on three occasions. Times he claimed to have lost time occurred during a canoe trip, while driving at night and during what he perceived as a nightmare. During his encounter when driving at night, he remembers not being able to see street or vehicle lights, and when he came to, he realized he had lost almost five hours.

Locals and UFO enthusiasts made the trek to Shoreline Park in Gulf Breeze in the hopes of seeing one of these mysterious lights in the sky. However, they could be making the journey to Florida's UFO Mecca based on a hoax.

Pensacola News Journal reporter Craig Myers[8] wrote and published a story about a model that resembles the UFOs seen in Walters's photos. The model was made from four plastic foam plates and pieces of drafting paper, and it was discovered in Walters's former Gulf Breeze home. A lot of controversy occurred over this discovery, but Walters stuck to his story, claiming everything he stated and reported was true.

Walters refused to take a polygraph test, but he did write and sign a sworn statement denying any knowledge of the UFO model found in his former home, which he moved out of in 1988. The new homeowner also wrote and signed a statement claiming he did not know who made the UFO model or how it got into his attic.

The model was nine inches across and five inches deep, with a six-inch orange paper ring and a blue plastic film to create a simulated blue beam of light. On the inside of the model, written on the drafting paper, were handwritten dimensions for a house on Jamestown Drive, which were in Walters's handwriting. It is known and documented by Santa Rosa County building permits that Walters built at least two homes on Jamestown Drive.

Once the model was discovered, the *News Journal* experimented to see if they could replicate the photos Walters presented as evidence of his alien abductions and encounters. The newspaper's photographers were able to nearly duplicate some of the pictures Walters gave in his book.

Many years later, Walters told the *News Journal* his wife was informed by a neighbor that a strange vehicle with out-of-state license plates entered the couple's garage. While in the garage, these mysterious strangers pulled down the attic stairs, entered the attic and suddenly left. The Gulf Breeze police were called and stated no break-in had occurred in the Walters's home.

Though many people still believe the Walters UFO incident was a hoax, UFO enthusiasts continue to visit the area in the hopes of seeing something strange in the skies above. A series of new sightings and renewed interest in Ufology spiked in the 1990s. In 1991, the Pensacola Bay Bridge saw an increase in visits from UFO enthusiasts who were armed with microphones and cameras.

In response to the sightings reported by Walters and the renewed interest and desire to see a UFO in the Gulf Breeze area, MUFON held its 1990 UFO Symposium near Pensacola. This event attracted hundreds of attendees, and the publicity attracted many more tourists and UFO sightseers throughout the following years.

BAREFOOT MAILMAN STATUE

HILLSBORO BEACH

One story shared among many living near the Hillsboro Inlet Lighthouse is about the Barefoot Mailman. This story is shared time and time again about the tragic event that occurred midway between Fort Lauderdale and Boca Raton in Hillsboro Beach. Though eleven barefoot mailmen worked in Hillsboro Beach, only one continues to live throughout history.

James "Ed" Hamilton was the area's barefoot mailman in the 1880s. He would walk throughout the community, and when needing to deliver mail to the Hillsboro Inlet Lighthouse, he would take a small rowboat he had left tied up on the shore across the inlet. A typical round-trip route for the barefoot mailman included traveling about eighty miles on foot and fifty-six miles by boat. It was a simple routine—until he arrived to deliver the mail one day and discovered that his rowboat was missing.

It is unsure what happened to his rowboat or who stole it, but it forced Hamilton to find a new way to fulfill his mailman duties. Since neither snow, rain, heat nor gloom of night stays these couriers from the swift completion of their appointed rounds, he knew he had only one choice—to swim across the inlet to the lighthouse.

What happened to Hamilton in 1887 when he was on his way to deliver the mail to the lighthouse remains a mystery. Since he braved the waters of the Hillsboro Inlet to deliver the mail, it is believed he was eaten by alligators, attacked by sharks or swept away by a strong current.

Hillsboro Inlet Light is located on the north side of Hillsboro Inlet, midway between Fort Lauderdale and Boca Raton, in Hillsboro Beach, Florida. *Carol M. Highsmith, Library of Congress.*

In 1973, a ten-foot-tall stone statue was erected in front of the Barefoot Mailman Hotel. When the hotel burned down, the town paid for the statue and relocated it in front of the municipal hall. Soon after, a second statue, this one made of bronze, was built and placed where the stone statue once stood because the original statue was relocated once again to the Coast Guard's Hillsboro Inlet Light Station. Here, the barefoot mailman's statue overlooks where Hamilton disappeared.

Throughout the years, people have reported seeing apparitions and shadowy figures walking along the beach where the barefoot mailman disappeared. Many believe that this ghostly figure is Hamilton as he continues to search for his missing boat and fulfill his mailman duties.

Captain Tony's

Key West

No trip to Key West is complete without a visit to Captain Tony's. This bar was once a morgue, and a hanging tree and gravestones, along with some lingering spirits, remain behind. The building has a long, macabre history dating back to the early nineteenth century.

One of the most unusual things about Captain Tony's is the gallows tree nestled inside the building that was constructed around it. This tree was used for judgments, and many pirates, runaway slaves and criminals met their end by hanging from this tree. More than seventy-five people met their fate from this tree, which passes through the roof of the restaurant and bar. Though some of the tree was lost to Hurricane Irma, you can still see about six inches of it peeking out above the building. But have no fear; this death tree is alive, as new twigs and leaves sprout inside the bar.

When the bar underwent renovations in the 1980s, approximately fifteen sets of bones were discovered under the floorboards. These eerie graves were implemented into the bar's design and can be seen while enjoying a beverage with friends or playing a game of pool.

One gravestone at Captain Tony's is of a young woman, Elvira Drew, who was married in her mid-teens to an abusive man in his fifties. She was hanged on the winter solstice at the age of nineteen in 1822 for killing her husband in self-defense. Today, her gravestone sits beside the pool table.

The gravestone of Reba I. Sawyer, a Key West native, sits underneath the old hanging tree. She died in 1950, and later, her husband found scandalous letters between her and another man. One letter described how they would meet at Captain Tony's Saloon. When her husband discovered this letter after her death, he dragged her tombstone from the cemetery into the bar, setting it under the tree. He claimed this was where his wife wanted to be and where she would stay for all eternity.

Captain Tony's Saloon at 428 Greene Street, Key West. *Dale M. McDonald, State Archives of Florida.*

There are many more bodies underneath the floor of Captain Tony's than there are gravestones. This makes visiting this restaurant eerie because you essentially walk over someone's grave wherever you are.

In addition to the eerie graves and thoughts about bodies lying underneath the floorboards, Captain Tony's is haunted by many spirits. The best-known spirit is the Lady in Blue. This apparition is often seen wearing a blood-soaked blue dress near the hanging tree. Frightened spectators call for help upon seeing her, including many who have reached the police, and upon further inspection, no one else is in the bar. Many paranormal investigators and enthusiasts have visited Captain Tony's, where they have seen and captured blue specters in photographs in the bar and claim this is the Lady in Blue who haunts the building.

The ladies' restroom is another location at Captain Tony's where people have had unexplainable encounters with the supernatural. Women who have used the restroom have reported being unable to unlock stall doors, having trouble keeping stall doors locked, hearing stall doors slam shut and stall doors mysteriously unlocking, opening and then slamming shut.

The bar's owner, Joe Farber, who calls himself a skeptic, encountered a voice calling for him at 4:00 a.m. one night. He got up to investigate and confirmed he was the only one in the bar, but he did notice the back doors were wide open. Farber knew he had locked the doors hours before and could not explain why the doors were open and where the voice came from.

Several years later, he heard the same voice call out for him when he was alone in the bar, but this time, the voice said, "Don't leave." One night, he believes it was a spirit telling him not to leave because there was a young girl who had taken pills to commit suicide. The young girl called her mother just after taking the pills, and Farber was called by the police shortly after because her body was found in front of Captain Tony's. Only the spirits know why they were calling out to Farber, but it was an eerie coincidence for him to hear the voice on this night.

Other reports of paranormal activity at Captain Tony's include cold spots, doors opening and closing, voices and apparitions lurking in the shadows. One patron reported suffering from third-degree burns after touching the hanging tree, but this has not been confirmed or backed by any evidence other than the witness's story.

Some people believe Captain Tony is behind some of the macabre decorations of the bar, placing gravestones in the bar and embellishing the decor with scary stories. Whether he created these stories or they are authentic, visiting Captain Tony's is a unique experience and provides many people the opportunity to witness paranormal activity.

DAMES POINT BRIDGE

JACKSONVILLE

Set on the I-295 East Beltway in Jacksonville, Florida, the Dames Point is one of the largest cable-stayed bridges in the United States. The bridge that crosses the St. Johns River was initially called the Napoleon Bonaparte Broward Bridge, after a local river pilot who eventually became governor of Florida. The Dames Point Bridge is a local icon, and people traveling through the area often go out of their way to glimpse this fantastic bridge.

In addition to being an impressive sight to see, the Dames Point Bridge is rumored to be the location where a young African American woman died after she was thrown over the bridge by an unknown assailant in 1996. Today, many people have reported seeing her spirit roaming the length of the bridge, and some have reported hearing disembodied cries.

The woman's apparition is not the only spirit rumored to be haunting the Dames Point Bridge. According to local legend, many people have intentionally jumped from the bridge and are now doomed to repeat the actions of their final moments in

Dames Point Bridge in Jacksonville. *James L. Gaines, State Archives of Florida.*

the afterlife. People have heard disembodied screams and cries and spotted shadow figures and faint apparitions of people appearing in emotional distress jumping over the side of the bridge.

Outside of a few stories shared online and among local paranormal investigators, not much else, paranormally speaking, happens at this roadside attraction. Either way, it is worth the visit; a spirit might make their presence known to a lucky visitor.

KEY WEST CEMETERY

KEY WEST

Many things about the Key West Cemetery are odd and unique. As it has everything from being the final resting place for historical figures to wacky epitaphs, this roadside attraction is one of the most visited locations in Key West, Florida. Strolling through the cemetery is like exploring a small city with quirky residents, heavy crowds and a colorful history.

Set in the center of Old Town, the Key West Cemetery has multiple entrances, with the best place to start exploring the cemetery from the entrance at the northwest corner at Passover Lane and Angela Street. This entrance has a small office and offers free guided walking tours. However, visitors are always invited to explore the cemetery on their own.

The cemetery is home to in-ground and aboveground graves and historic statues; the high water table could be a factor for many who chose the aboveground option. Additionally, the aboveground graves offer extra space in the cemetery because it is possible to have three aboveground graves in place of two underground vaults.

Unfortunately, this cemetery, which was founded in 1847, was devastated by a hurricane in October 1846, which washed away much of the old cemetery, scattering bodies throughout a nearby forest. Because of this, the oldest gravestones in the graveyard to survive were set at the highest point in the area, with graves dating back to 1829 and 1843. These older headstones were relocated to the cemetery after the hurricane.

Some have claimed their feeling when visiting the Key West Cemetery is similar to the one in New Orleans. Everything from the aboveground crypts

The *Maine* monument in the Key West city cemetery. *State Archives of Florida.*

to the eerie feelings and the ghosts and local legends creates a similar feeling when walking among the dead at this historical and must-visit Florida cemetery.

Exploring the Key West Cemetery takes visitors along a path similar to a small town with narrow streets, but instead of homes and businesses, there are rows of whitewashed headstones lining the paths. And instead of people, chickens, iguanas and ghosts are lingering around every corner.

Spirits that are reported to remain behind haunting the Key West Cemetery include a Bahamian woman believed to oversee the cemetery in the afterlife, approaching visitors who are not respecting or are caught sitting on the graves. Her spirit is joined by the spirits of some of the more than seventy thousand people buried in the Key West Cemetery. Many visitors to the cemetery have reported seeing light anomalies, shadows and full-bodied apparitions as they explore the mysterious cemetery.

In addition to the many lost souls remaining to roam the Key West Cemetery grounds, many unique and intriguing headstones and statues are scattered throughout. One interesting headstone reads, "I told you I was sick," belonging to hypochondriac B.P. "Pearl" Roberts. Another one everyone seems to talk about claims the person buried underneath was a "Devoted fan of Singer Julio Iglesias." The headstone belongs to local barkeep "Sloppy" Joe Russel, stating, "I'm just resting my eyes."

These unique headstone engravings can be found throughout the cemetery, but one of the most interesting graves is that of Archibald John Sheldon Yates. His grave is adorned with a statue of a nude woman whose hands are tied behind her back. This grave is a long-standing mystery, and Key West visitors and locals have yet to unlock its story. Local legend does claim the figure is of his wife, Magdalena, and represents something other than grief. For some reason, Yates wanted her on his grave, naked, and there she sat. The statue of the naked bound woman has become a roadside attraction of its own, and many visitors to the Key West Cemetery are there to see her.

Six-Toed Cats
of Ernest Hemingway

Key West

Key West is indeed home to some of the most strange and mysterious roadside attractions, but one must-see attraction is stopping by the Ernest Hemingway House and Museum to see descendants of his six-toed cat named Snowy. The furry four-legged residents are the main attraction for many coming to Key West, and while exploring Hemingway's home and museum, you can spot cats stretching out on benches and by the pool. Some of these cats have been spotted climbing and roosting in the palm trees scattered throughout the property.

So why does the Ernest Hemingway House and Museum have over forty resident cats? Here's what local legend has to say about this.

The legacy of Hemingway's six-toed cats all started with one. Captain Stanley Dexter gave Hemingway a white six-toed kitten after the author had admired the captain's six-toed cat. Hemingway's new feline was named Snow White after the famous storybook character. After that, Hemingway named all his cats after famous people and fictional characters, such as Willard Scott, Errol Flynn and Gremlin.

Though the original six-toed cats have died, the museum honors this tradition by providing a home for these cats, many of whom (but not all) are descendants of Snow White. The

Opposite: Ernest Hemingway seated at a typewriter. *Arnold R. Lloyd, Library of Congress.*

Right: Cats lying by the fountain at the Ernest Hemingway House and Museum in Key West. *State Archives of Florida.*

Below: Ernest Hemingway's home in Key West. *Carol M. Highsmith, Library of Congress.*

Hemingway House and Museum currently has six-toed cats named Lucille Ball, "Sloppy" Joe Russel, Jackie O, Ginger Rogers and Alfred Hitchcock. All cats residing at this roadside attraction in Key West have unique personalities and quirky traits.

Like most of Key West, the Hemingway House and Museum is no stranger to paranormal activity. Many people have reported seeing Papa Hemingway haunting the halls and grounds of his former home and his precious feline friends. Guests of the house have reported being woken up in the middle of the night by a black-and-white tuxedo cat that would jump on their bed and sit at the foot, staring at them. One guest reported feeling paws walking across his chest, and when he opened his eyes, no cat was present. Some visitors have approached cats on the grounds, and they meowed and purred as they were petted before vanishing.

In addition to seeing and hearing Hemingway's cats, many have reported strange paranormal events believed to be linked to the writer. The sounds of a typewriter clicking and clacking away and sounds of papers shuffling can be heard, and brief moments have been reported where visitors see Hemingway sitting at his desk writing or standing on the balcony overlooking the garden.

Outside of the home's beautiful construction, design and decor, the Hemingway House and Museum is one place in Key West to explore when seeking interactions with supernatural entities.

TRUMAN'S LITTLE WHITE HOUSE

KEY WEST

E ven U.S. presidents need a vacation, and President Harry Truman's favorite vacation destination was the Florida Keys. This once vice president (who became president after the death of President Franklin D. Roosevelt in 1945) had a vacation home nestled in the Sunshine State, where he spent many vacations relaxing and taking a break from his hectic presidential lifestyle. Truman's doctor ordered him to take a break to recoup from nineteen months of strenuous decision-making, including the use of the atomic bombs on Hiroshima and Nagasaki.

Unlike typical Florida landscaping, Truman's Little White House remains in Key West. This darling structure is popular for weddings, history buffs and Key West visitors to explore and learn more about Truman's activities in the Sunshine State. And yes, Truman's Little White House is haunted.

What is known today as his Little White House was once part of the navy barracks, but he loved the area and turned the barracks into his vacation home. Truman visited the area eleven times, totaling 175 days during his presidency, and often called Key West his second-favorite place on Earth, just after Independence, Missouri, his hometown.

In Key West, Truman was known for kicking off his shoes, loosening his belt and relaxing. During his getaways to the Little White House, Truman did not have to be as uptight as he felt during his presidential duties, and he could escape the pressure of making life-altering decisions.

The Little White House was visited and used by at least six U.S. presidents, but Truman fell in love with the property. Because of his love,

Truman's "Little White House," Key West. *Carol M. Highsmith, Library of Congress.*

most of what is found in the museum connects with Truman and his life as president and in Key West.

Entering through the front door is like stepping through a portal in time. When visitors reach the other side of the threshold, they are taken back to a time when Truman visited, and many believe he is still there, soaking up the sun and taking a break from being president.

Though Truman's Little White House is haunted, the resident ghost is not the former president. It is unknown who this spirit is, but employees and visitors have reported coming face to face with full-bodied apparitions in the house museum. Some employees believe there is also the spirit of a former employee who still reports for duty monitoring the museum halls in the afterlife.

It is also believed that some spirits haunting Truman's Little White House are naval officers, guests and vacationers who fell in love with the home as much as Truman did. Some employees believe that one of the entities haunting the home and museum is a former house manager because while they are working, they feel a strong presence watching over them, ensuring they get their jobs done right.

Several spirits at Truman's Little White House are intelligent, meaning they respond and interact with people in the home and museum. Still, much more paranormal activity is happening that is believed to be residual. With so many spirits and strong feelings, many employees have quit to avoid the unnerving sensation they feel inside the home. Whether residual or intelligent, there is something creepy happening within the walls of this historic Key West home.

Forgotten Citrus Center Monuments

#1 Lumberton
#3 Lakeland

There are multiple towers throughout Polk County, and few residents know what they are for. Around 1930, several of these large concrete markers were placed at the entry points of Polk County, welcoming visitors to Florida's "Citrus Center." Two of the three remaining Citrus Center monuments are the sites of unexplained occurrences with no known origins.

The Lumberton monument (#1) is set on US 98 near the intersection with Highway 54. This towering concrete monument is set off the side of the road in front of an open field, with plenty of space to pull over and admire the massive structure. It is unknown if this monument is haunted by the spirit of someone who died nearby or if it is just a hitchhiking ghost trying to get back to Orlando. Many have seen what appears to be someone walking on the side of the road, but when they look in the rearview mirror, no one is there. With nothing but open roads and fields, it would be near impossible for someone walking along the road to find a place to hide in the split second it takes to pass them driving sixty miles per hour.

The Lakeland monument (#3) is set at a bustling, dangerous intersection on County Line Road, standing next to railroad tracks. Those who have braved trying to stop by this monument have seen apparitions and shadow people walking along the tracks. The area could attract these spirits because many believe paranormal activity is heightened around railroad tracks. Others feel that the spirits lingering in this area are those who fell victim to a car accident, hit-and-run or collision with a train.

Polk County Citrus Marker #1 in Lumberton, Florida, which marked one of the entry points into the county. *By Heather Leigh, PhD.*

Though there are claims that these monuments are haunted or have spirits hanging around in the area, there are no public reports of paranormal investigations conducted at either.

WORLD'S LARGEST BUFFALO CHICKEN WING

MADEIRA BEACH

J ohn's Pass is a small fishing village that is a tourist attraction and home to one of the most exciting roadside attractions in Southwest Florida. Hanging proudly as if it were caught at sea is the world's largest buffalo chicken wing, seen from Hooters patio restaurant.

Though the chicken wing is not haunted, there are legends of Confederate soldiers who hike the nearby bridge, and chatter from performing dolphins is heard across the bay. John's Pass is one of the most haunted locations in the area and is visited by paranormal researchers in the hopes of unlocking answers to the supernatural.

When dining at Hooters, guests have a fantastic view of the John's Pass Drawbridge, where spirits of two Confederate soldiers are spotted walking over the bridge. Who are these mysterious soldiers? Locals have many stories that could identify these ghostly apparitions and why they continue to step back and forth across the bridge.

Many believe these are the apparitions of two soldiers who lived in the area before heading to war. In contrast, others believe the spirits may be those of two soldiers who deserted their fellow soldiers to return to Florida. Upon their return home, the local Rebel militia hunted them down and murdered them for their cowardly acts.

One local legend claims these two ghosts are not Confederate soldiers but two local farmers who were pro-Union during the Civil War. Local Rebel militiamen murdered the two farmers and buried their bodies on the southern end of the pass's mouth. The two farmers are spotted walking the

The World's Largest Chicken Wing found outside Hooters Restaurant at John's Pass in Madeira Beach. *By Heather Leigh, PhD.*

bridge when there is a full moon. Some also claim they have spotted these spirits silently sailing through the area, and a strong smell of decaying flesh is inhaled as the boat passes by.

Joined by the ghostly images of the soldiers crossing over the drawbridge, there are rumors that the energy from Patty, Mike and Frank, the performing dolphins at the Marine Arena across the pass, can be heard outside the closed arena's walls. The Marine Arena was a popular attraction in the Madeira Beach area but fell upon hard times in the 1960s, which forced the owners to ship Frank and Mike to another aquarium. The loss of Mike and Frank was more than Patty could handle, especially since the dolphin was left behind to

The bridge as seen from Hooters Restaurant at John's Pass in Madeira Beach. *By Heather Leigh, PhD.*

carry on in isolation. The Marine Arena officially closed in the 1970s, and since then, passersby of the shuttered structure have heard echoes of the squeals of Patty crying for her lost mates. This is a sad story that tugs at the heartstrings of many, and if Patty's spirit remains behind, it must be lonely for her to continue living in isolation in the afterlife.

John's Pass has many thrilling stories about spirits and local legends that are scary enough to give someone goosebumps. Stopping by to admire the world's largest buffalo chicken wing puts visitors in the heart of much of the paranormal activity at this fun and active fishing village.

Daffodale House
Bed and Breakfast

Monticello

T he Daffodale House Bed and Breakfast is one of the most haunted inns in the country, nestled in one of the most haunted towns in the South. Those who dare to spend the night report encountering shadow figures, experiencing apparitions and hearing disembodied voices emanating from the town's past, which stretches back to the early nineteenth century.

Visitors have often been swept away in thought as they admire the unique, charming exterior of the Daffodale House Bed and Breakfast and then get swept away when they see the delightfully decorated interior. But nothing knocks guests off their feet more than the many ghosts who also reside within the walls of this quaint Florida bed-and-breakfast.

As soon as you step through the front doors, the structure and its resident spirits start to share and retell stories from Monticello's past. This home, built in 1897, has many hauntings that were first discovered by owners the Ebberbachs. When in the home, the owners heard strange music coming from within rooms with no guests, and aromas of pipe smoking appeared in areas where no one was smoking.

Other unexplainable occurrences within the walls of the Daffodale House include lighting turning on and off on its own and items disappearing and then reappearing in guest rooms. Some guests have come face to face with the woman in white, who is often spotted roaming the grounds of the bed-and-breakfast at night.

Paranormal researchers who have investigated the house felt that most of the paranormal activity comes from the attic. It is believed that the spirits of an entire family continue to live their afterlife hanging out in the attic of this beautiful home. Evidence of paranormal activity in the attic includes hearing disembodied voices, seeing shadow figures and experiencing a strong feeling of not being alone.

Many believe the spirits and related paranormal activity at this location are tied to the several artifacts, statues and relics containing pieces of history from Monticello and other nearby areas in Florida and worldwide. The most intriguing of these artifacts is the bronzed death mask lining the shelves. Creepy as it might be to some, there is nothing to fear from what may be attached to this death mask because no negative energies have been reported residing at the Daffodale House Bed and Breakfast.

SUGAR MILL RUINS

NEW SMYRNA BEACH

A hidden, haunted treasure in New Smyrna Beach, Florida, is the Sugar Mill Ruins, once part of the Cruger-dePeyster Plantation. The plantation was built in the early nineteenth century. It has seventeen acres and contains a coquina sugar factory. Built around 1830, this property holds an interesting legend claiming the sugar mill was built on top of the site where a chapel built by Christopher Columbus once stood.[9]

This area of New Smyrna Beach was a much-desired location, and the addition of the sugar mill made it the target of raids during the war between the United States and the Seminole Indians. During this attack, many structures on the plantation, including the sugar mill, were destroyed. After the attacks, soldiers were sent to protect the plantation and surrounding homes and businesses in New Smyrna Beach. However, upon inspection, the sugar mill was beyond saving and left in ruins.

In 1970, the plantation and sugar mill ruins were listed on the National Register of Historic Places. It has been a popular place for people to visit to learn more about history and see if they can encounter a spirit from the past.

Today, the ruins are rumored to be haunted by the spirits of Seminole Indians, who can be seen running through the woods in the early morning hours. Joining these spirits are shadow people who mostly appear near sunset, darting behind trees in the forest and the ruins.

Many people have felt an evil presence when exploring the sugar mill ruins, including being watched and followed. Those who claim there is an

This page: New Smyrna Sugar Mill (ruins), New Smyrna (historical), Volusia County. *Library of Congress.*

evil presence believe so because they feel incredibly uncomfortable, and some have had to leave the area because of heightened anxiety and a sense of fear.

The sugar mill ruins are a must-experience for anyone looking to catch a glimpse of the past. Plus, this is a great location to catch a glimpse of a spirit or two lurking in the shadows.

Oldest Building in Western Hemisphere

North Miami Beach

Accoording to historical records, the Ancient Spanish Monastery in North Miami Beach is the oldest European-constructed building in the Western Hemisphere.[10] The idea that this structure is the oldest in the hemisphere is a bit of a struggle for many because St. Augustine was founded in 1565, and many older structures are found in Old San Juan, Puerto Rico, and Havana, Cuba.

Though other countries have been around longer than many of Florida's communities, there is an answer why this popular roadside attraction has been dubbed the oldest building in the Western Hemisphere. Even more interesting is that this structure is not what is expected when visiting an old monastery and is more similar to seeing the ancient ruins of the Aztecs and Incas.

The Ancient Spanish Monastery was constructed in 1141 in Sacramenia, in northern Spain near Segovia. The building was initially named the Monastery of Our Lady, Queen of Angels. Later, the monastery was renamed Bernard of Clairvaux after the newly canonized saint. As a Cistercian monk, Bernard and his fellow monks called the monastery home for the next seven hundred years.

When revolution struck Spain in the 1830s, the monastery's cloisters and other on-site structures were seized, sold and eventually repurposed into a granary and stable.

In 1925, William Randolph Hearst, a famous and wealthy newspaper owner in the United States, bought the cloisters and the outbuildings. He planned to have the buildings taken apart, brick by brick, and then wrapped in hay for protection and packed into more than eleven thousand wooden crates. The brick-filled crates were shipped to the United States and stored in a Brooklyn, New York warehouse. They remained in storage until Hearst died in 1952, when they were sold to a group that wanted to use the bricks to create a tourist attraction.

Two years and millions of dollars later, the structures were put back together in what *Time* magazine called "the biggest jigsaw puzzle in history." In 1964, Colonel Robert Pentland Jr. purchased the cloisters as a gift for the bishop of Florida, and the structure became an active congregation of the Episcopal Diocese of Southeast Florida.

When visiting the ancient monastery, visitors claim to see shadow figures, see light anomalies, hear disembodied voices and experience strange encounters.

Many people love to stop by and visit the Ancient Spanish Monastery for its beautiful architecture. They also enjoy getting lost in the peaceful halls as they walk the property among the ghosts of medieval Spain.

MA BARKER'S HOUSE

OCKLAWAHA

Consider this your ghostly warning: beware of Ma Barker because she is not happy and is letting everyone know well after she has passed.

Ma Barker's House is known as the Historic Bradford House in Ocklawaha, Florida, and is the site of the 1935 FBI shootout with the Barker gang. Visitors can see bullet holes that have been poorly patched throughout when visiting the two-story home. This home is haunted by Ma Barker, who remains behind in the afterlife, protecting her home.

Ma Barker, born Kate Barker on October 8, 1873, was the matriarch of a gang of American hoodlums known as the infamous Barker-Karpis gang. This gang rose to notoriety during the public enemy era, when many other gangs, mobsters and killers were attracting the attention of the people, press and FBI. Like many other gangs during this era, the Barker-Karpis gang rose to a high level of popularity quickly, which aided in its demise.

Barker rose to fame and is best known for her role as the brutal crime queen because she managed and directed her sons to create offenses that were vicious and dangerous. For years, the gang wreaked havoc on the public, landing many of them in jail during their reign of terror.

Due to all the media and law enforcement attention the gang had captured, they fled to Florida. Eventually, the gang holed up in a small shack nestled on the outskirts of Ocala, but they could not hide for long.

Eventually, the FBI caught up to them using new forensic technology. On January 16, 1935, FBI agents circled the home where Ma Barker and her gang hid. When the agents arrived, Ma and her son Fred were the only ones in the house. The rest of the gang had gone out of town.

During the volley of more than two thousand bullets from the Barker gang and federal agents, the house was nearly torn to shreds. The shootout lasted for hours, and several locals stopped by to watch the tragic events unfold. In the end, Fred's body was riddled with bullets, while Ma died from a single gunshot wound.

After the shootout, the bodies of Ma and Fred were put on display and then stored until October 1, 1935. Eventually, the two were buried at Williams Timberhill Cemetery in Welch, Oklahoma, next to the body of Herman Barker, another of Ma's sons.

The horrific events that occurred during the shootout with federal agents left a significant imprint on the environment of the home and surrounding land. Many paranormal investigators have claimed to have encountered the spirit of Ma Barker, who is believed to be haunting the house where she and her son spent their final days.

Many people who have visited the Barker gang's former estate have shared numerous stories about coming face to face with Ma Barker. Some paranormal investigators have called the property a "storm of paranormal activity."

Ma doesn't like people touching her belongings or her home and despises the idea of northern snowbirds coming into her house or even attempting to relocate the property elsewhere. One investigator, a retired police patrolman from upstate New York, claimed to hear a snarling voice yelling at him when he was beneath the live oaks after touring the home: "Get outta here, lawman!" He fled in fright but believed it was Ma giving him a warning.

Others who have visited the home have left pale as a ghost or come running out, claiming they will never return. But what happens in the house to scare so many people away? Who knows, because not many will speak of what happens and forever hold the secret of the hauntings of the Barker gang.

TITANIC: THE EXPERIENCE

ORLANDO

The tragedy from the 1912 events when the *Titanic* sank in the Atlantic live on at Titanic: The Experience in Orlando, Florida. Many believe the spirits of those who perished as the ship sank beneath the water's surface remain behind to haunt the many artifacts on display at this popular Central Florida attraction.

Titanic: The Experience is an immersive and poignant journey into the captivating story of the RMS *Titanic*. Located in the heart of Orlando, this exhibit transports visitors to the fateful night of April 14, 1912, when the "unsinkable" ship met its tragic end.

Upon entering the exhibit, you are greeted with a replica of the grand staircase, mirroring the luxury of the original ship. The ambiance echoes with the sounds of a bygone era, creating an authentic atmosphere that sets the stage for your exploration. Marvel at meticulously restored artifacts recovered from the ocean floor, each telling a unique tale of the passengers and crew. From personal belongings to the ship's china and silverware, every item on display provides a tangible connection to the people who sailed on the ill-fated voyage.

The exhibit employs cutting-edge technology to bring history to life. Walk through intricately reconstructed cabins and witness the challenges those aboard the *Titanic* faced. Experience the chilling temperature of the iceberg-filled waters through interactive displays, allowing you to understand the harsh realities of that tragic night.

One of the highlights is a full-scale replica of a lifeboat, giving visitors a sense of the limited space and difficult decisions survivors faced. Engage with knowledgeable guides who share gripping stories of heroism and heartbreak, providing a deeper understanding of the human stories behind the disaster.

For a truly immersive experience, step into the memorial room dedicated to honoring the lives lost during the *Titanic*'s sinking. Reflect on the impact of this historic event and pay tribute to the passengers and crew who perished.

Titanic: The Experience in Orlando offers a thought-provoking and emotionally resonant exploration of one of history's most infamous maritime tragedies. Whether you're a history enthusiast, curious about this iconic event or a paranormal researcher, this exhibit invites you to delve into the past and remember the legacy of the *Titanic*.

It is a very eerie feeling wandering through this exhibit, especially when you are struck with a cool spot, see shadow figures or feel like you are being followed from room to room. Employees and visitors believe there is conclusive evidence that these ghostly friends from the *Titanic* are hanging around their beloved belongings.

Employees have reported seeing strange occurrences during nearly every shift they work. Some of the activities experienced include moving artifacts, items disappearing and reappearing elsewhere in the museum and disembodied voices. Photographic evidence has also been captured, including the image of transparent legs that appear to belong to a crew member.

With multiple paranormal events experienced and captured, Titanic: The Experience is haunted by the passengers and crew members who perished on that tragic day. Whatever happens within the exhibit's walls is often up for debate, but there is no denying several unusual events and strange occurrences happen at this exhibit.

FAIRCHILD OAK

ORMOND BEACH

Ormond Beach, Florida, is home to many mysteries and legends, but one roadside attraction holds a legend of two deaths and sits in what is today a picturesque park. The Fairchild Oak is nestled in Bulow Creek State Park and is one of the most enormous live oaks in the southeastern United States. The live oak has been watching over Bulow Creek for over four hundred years and has witnessed many events throughout the area. While guarding the area's magnificent environment, Fairchild Oak survived when the neighboring Bulow Plantation was destroyed during the Second Seminole War in 1836.

The first death Fairchild Oak witnessed was of James Ormond II. Ormond lived in a home just a stone's throw from the tree, and his body was found underneath the tree. The cause of death was unknown, and it remains a mystery.

Ormond's father, James Ormond, purchased the 1,687-acre plantation known as Damietta to grow sugar, cotton and indigo. A runaway slave killed his father, and the family briefly moved back to Scotland. But Ormond returned to the plantation with his wife and four children in 1820. The family abandoned the plantation when Ormond Jr. was killed in 1829 and never returned.

The second death was even more mysterious. Norman Harwood purchased the property around 1880, and many people claim he was a cattle farmer, while others say he was a dry-goods businessman. No matter his profession, Harwood was known to be deep in debt caused by excessive spending. Eventually, the Panic of 1873 forced him to lose everything and left him in debt for almost $2 million.

His death remains a mystery, but many speculate he killed himself underneath the tree because of the economic turmoil he brought upon himself. Other reports claim that on May 15, 1885, Harwood was out riding his horse when he was found dead after apparently falling off. Since he had a life insurance policy worth more than $200,000, many people speculate his death was not an accident.

It is also rumored that since Harwood's death, several people have made their way to the live oak to end their lives. Because of this, Fairchild Oak is often referred to as the Suicide Tree. However, there are no confirmed reports of these additional deaths underneath Fairchild Oak.

Fairchild Oak is a beautiful site, and many hikers head to the tree to see fantastic wildlife, including birds, white-tailed deer, raccoons and barred owls. Paranormal investigators make their way to the tree for an opportunity to encounter the apparition of a man often spotted sitting under the tree with a look of sorrow on his face.

If you take the time to sit underneath Fairchild Oak and enjoy the beauty of the surrounding area, you may hear the whispers of the spirits who remain behind. Other reports of unexplainable activity near the tree include being touched, feeling the sudden onset of migraine pain and seeing shadow figures walking in the distance as if they are watching over the tree.

Whether the legends are true or the paranormal activity is the result of the stories being shared throughout generations and the activity manifesting throughout the years, no doubt unexplained events happen when near Fairchild Oak.

Oviedo Ghost Lights

Oviedo

One eerie legend Florida is known worldwide for is the mysterious Oviedo Ghost Lights. The small town of Oviedo, just outside Orlando, is best known for its natural beauty, wilderness spots and winding hiking trails, but it is also home to some of the most mysterious and famous folklore Florida has to tell. Not only is this small town known for having some fantastic historic homes and buildings, but the legend of the Oviedo Lights is extraordinary.

According to legend, people crossing the bridge over the Econlockhatchee River near Chuluota and Snow Hill's intersection see a weird, greenish glowing set of lights. It appears these glowing light anomalies rise out of the surrounding swamp and murky river waters up toward the bridge. This was a popular teen hangout between the 1940s and the 1970s, with the lights being more active during the warmer months.

Some people have said these are fireflies or a trick of the eye, but reports about these lights go back more than fifty years, and several people have reported seeing them come up to the bridge and chase after vehicles. Many locals believed swamp gas was causing the lights until they witnessed the lights chase after a car.

However, the idea that swamp gases cause these lights is a scientific explanation behind these lights. When the methane and phosphines of the swamp gas self-ignite when they come in contact with oxygen, it creates spontaneous bursts of light. Swamp gases can produce strange light anomalies, also known as jack-o'-lanterns, will-o'-wisps or swamp ghost lights; when created and combined with scary legends, they can cause people to see phenomena similar to the Oviedo ghost lights.

In 1969, students from the University of Central Florida's physics department were tasked to examine, study and research the lights. Upon the completion of the study, the university released a statement: "insufficient information on which to base a concrete scientific opinion."[11]

Stories about the lights vary, especially regarding the number of lights. Many people report seeing only one light coming up from below, while others have reported seeing as many as five appear simultaneously.

The Oviedo ghost lights have become a popular Central Florida attraction, with many courageous visitors venturing out at night with a flashlight, hoping to find them on a dark, foggy night.

FLAGLER MUSEUM—GOLD TELEGRAM

PALM BEACH

Henry Flagler is an essential historical figure in Florida, with many roadside attractions dedicated to his memory and accomplishments. Many historians credit Flagler as the founder of Palm Beach, where Whitehall was built. Whitehall is a seventy-five-room mansion Flagler constructed as a wedding gift for his wife, Mary Lily Kenan. The couple intended to use the residence as their winter home, but they stayed in Florida once they moved into the house on February 6, 1902.

Flagler died at eighty-three in 1913 after completing his dream of building a railroad from Palm Beach to Key West. Mary died four years later, and their home was turned into the Flagler Museum. The spirits of Flagler and his wife have been spotted in the house, enjoying their time entertaining visitors. Employees have reported unexplainable damage to artifacts and doors refusing to open, and one cleaning lady claimed to be slapped on the bottom by whom she believed to be Flagler.

In addition to Mr. and Mrs. Flagler haunting the museum, several visitors have reported strange activity near the gold telegram. Rumors and stories told in Palm Beach's whispers claim a spirit lurks in the shadows near the gold telegram. Visitors and employees have reported experiencing the sensation of being watched, being touched on the shoulder and hearing disembodied voices when near this famous artifact in the museum.

Through artifacts and imagery chronicling Henry Flagler's life and achievements, the Flagler Kenan History Room offers visitors a compelling glimpse into his legacy. As a pivotal figure in the founding of the Standard

Henry M. Flagler Mansion, Whitehall Way, Palm Beach. *Historic American Buildings Survey.*

Oil Company and a paramount developer in Florida, Flagler's impact is vividly portrayed. One notable exhibit is an eighteen-karat gold replica of the Western Union telegram that heralded the completion of the Key West Extension. Crafted by Tiffany & Co., the original telegram and its ornate gold box, adorned with motifs reflecting Florida and the railroad, were presented to Flagler by grateful employees during the dedication of the Over-Sea Railroad in 1912. Complementing this centerpiece are a wealth of artifacts associated with Mary Lily Kenan Flagler and the esteemed Kenan family, enriching the historical tapestry of the room.

As visitors immerse themselves in the exhibits, a subtle ambiance envelops the Flagler Kenan History Room. Phantom clicking noises, reminiscent of the dot-dot-dash rhythm of telegrams being sent from a bygone era, echo through the space. These spectral sounds serve as a haunting reminder of Flagler's pivotal role in communication and transportation history, evoking a sense of connection to the past that permeates the room.

Reports of paranormal activity are near the telegram and throughout the Flagler Museum. Other supernatural activity accounts include hearing footsteps when no one is walking, capturing faces in windows in photographs and experiencing strange smells and unexplainable temperature drops.

Is it possible that Whitehall Mansion and the Flagler Museum are haunted? Anything is possible, and those who have visited the museum or worked there have claimed it is one of the most active locations in Palm Beach.

GOLD COAST RAILROAD MUSEUM

MIAMI

The building housing the Gold Coast Railroad Museum dates back to World War II, when it was a naval base. The Naval Air Station Richmond opened on September 15, 1942, and became the Gold Coast Railroad Museum in 1956. The museum was one of three Official State Railroad Museums in Florida, and in 1984, the museum was relocated to Hangar #1 and Hangar #2. These hangars were once used to house blimps during the war.

Once the former naval air station was transformed into a museum, it started collecting and acquiring several pieces of railroad history, including steamers, passenger cars, segregated cars and medical cars. The museum was dedicated to preserving railroad history, and it quickly acquired more than forty historic railcars, including the Western Pacific "Silver Crescent" and engines such as Florida East Coast 113.

The Gold Coast Railroad Museum's pride and joy is the presidential car named the Ferdinand Magellan, also known as Presidential Railcar No. 1. The fully armored car transported presidents, including Roosevelt, Truman and Eisenhower. Though it was retired, the railcar was brought out of retirement to serve as a prop in the 1980s for Reagan's presidential reelection campaign.

Visitors, employees and paranormal researchers who have visited the Gold Coast Railroad Museum have reported many experiences, including an angry spirit that yells, "Get out!" In addition to the disgruntled spirit, the disembodied voices of a female and several children have been captured

A railroad station and car of the Gold Coast Railroad Museum, Fort Lauderdale. *State Archives of Florida.*

during EVP sessions, strange noises happen throughout the museum and one spirit likes to repeat profanities. Several people have reported being touched by something unseen in the Old Machine Shop.

Additionally, various investigation tools, such as REM Pods, EDI+ and K2 Meters, go off randomly without rhyme or reason. It almost appears these devices are malfunctioning, which is possible, but some researchers believe it to be the spirits messing with them in hopes the investigators leave.

Fort Barrancas—Old Tunnels

Pensacola

Designed to stop foreign invasion, Fort Barrancas is a naval air station overlooking Pensacola Bay, which saw military action only during the American Civil War. After the war, the fort continued to serve as part of the United States' coast defense system until it became part of Pensacola Naval Air Station in 1947.

Fort Barrancas was expanded to connect with the Spanish-built water battery through an underground walkway tunnel. These tunnels were designed by Joseph Gilbert Totten, and Major William Henry Chase supervised the construction, which was completed mainly using enslaved African American workers.

What was once a piece of Florida history is now one of the most haunted locations in Pensacola. Paranormal investigators, researchers and experiencers have reported many strange occurrences happening throughout Fort Barrancas, especially in the tunnels. These ghostly experiences are supported by information, stories and details shared by visitors to the fort and employees who work and have worked at Fort Barrancas.

Paranormal experiences within the tunnels at Fort Barrancas include everything from sudden barometric pressure changes to the sensation of someone standing behind a person and sounds of footsteps to seeing shadow figures standing greater than six feet tall. One spirit, a Confederate soldier, is often spotted walking the tunnels. Some believe this is a residual haunting, as the apparition goes about his business as if no one else is around him.

Barracks at
Fort Barrancas,
Pensacola. *Detroit
Publishing Co.*

There is another apparition of a Confederate soldier spotted throughout the fort, which is believed to be that of one of two men who were executed on the fort grounds. According to legend, the soldier was hanged because he fell asleep while on guard duty. The soldier wandering fort grounds may be the same as the one spotted inside the tunnels. Some believe the soldier's spirit in the tunnel is performing his duties for all eternity as punishment for failing to fulfill his military duties when alive.

FANTASY OF FLIGHT MUSEUM

POLK CITY

Anyone who has driven along I-4 traveling between Orlando and Tampa has passed the infamous plane sitting on the side of the road. Many moons ago, the aircraft had a mannequin of a pilot hanging out the side door, waving at passing traffic. Though the mannequin is no longer present, the museum of the plane advertised in Polk City remains a popular roadside attraction.

Fantasy of Flight Museum is home to the Kermit Weeks aircraft collection in Polk City, Florida, housing over forty fully restored vintage aircraft. The museum opened in 1995 and is the perfect place to visit for those who are passionate about aviation history and ghosts. The fleet of vintage aircraft has earned the admiration of knowledgeable aviators, inspired the imagination of those who dreamed of flying a plane and drawn paranormal investigators looking for answers to some of the most challenging supernatural questions.

Visitors and employees have experienced strange occurrences since Fantasy of Flight opened its doors to the first visitors. The most common experiences include hearing unidentifiable noises and encountering unexplainable, drastic temperature changes. Visitors have captured apparitions in photographs within the area where the planes are on display, and security cameras have captured strange and unexplainable mists and shadows. Though rare, some have reported face-to-face encounters with spirits that are believed to be connected to the aircraft housed at the museum.

Could the spirits be attached to the planes and artifacts at Fantasy of Flight? Or could they be related to the history of the land and environment the museum sits on? Anything is possible, and many paranormal researchers believe it is a combination of the two possibilities.

LAST RESORT BAR

PORT ORANGE

Set in the small town of Port Orange, Florida, the Last Resort is a biker bar with ties to a serial killer who was convicted and executed. The Last Resort Bar was the last place Aileen "Monster" Wuornos visited before being arrested for the murders she committed. As a frequent visitor of the bar, Aileen is remembered by those who once hung around through the sale of T-shirts with the photo of her arrest at the bar. There is also a framed photo of her hanging on the bar wall, and they sell bottles of Crazed Killer Hot Sauce, her favorite condiment.

Aileen was arrested at the Last Resort Bar on January 8, 1991, after police were secretly watching her and hiding in the bar. On the night of her arrest, she was left by her lover and was in a position where she could no longer pay her twenty-five-dollar-per-night motel room. That night, she had no idea the police were watching her and they were about to execute an arrest warrant.

Aileen, a thirty-four-year-old sex worker, went to the bar to keep a low profile. She played pool with other patrons and added her bra to the rafters filled with women's undergarments. At the end of the evening, she passed out on the front porch of the Last Resort Bar and was approached by two undercover officers.

The officers offered to pay for a room for her, but instead, she was taken into custody for an outstanding warrant for possessing a concealed weapon. Later, during the same arrest, she was held and eventually convicted of six counts of first-degree murder. The murders were committed between 1989 and 1990, and Aileen claimed they were men who solicited her for sex, and she was not in agreement with what the men wanted.

Aileen earned the title of the FBI's first woman to be profiled as a serial killer and spent a decade on death row at the now-closed Broward Correctional Institution. During her time on death row, Aileen held on to her innocence, claiming she killed the men in self-defense because they raped or attempted to rape her because she did not agree to the terms of their sex-for-money agreement. Though Aileen continued to plead that she committed the murders in self-defense, she was not shy about claiming she would do it again if she were ever put in that position. Aileen was executed by lethal injection on October 9, 2002.

Almost immediately after her execution, staff and patrons of the Last Resort Bar started experiencing unexplainable paranormal activity. Women visiting the bar feel like someone is brushing their hair, and the bell rings now and then without explanation.

Then, one year around Oktoberfest, the bar had a dollar store skeleton hanging for decoration. The arm would continually fall off, and they would find it in strange places throughout the bar. It was always the left arm, and it is believed that this is because the lethal injection was put in Aileen's left arm.

One night, during a seance performed by an Australian paranormal team, video and photos captured strange shadows and light anomalies. Objects would disappear and reappear or move without human interaction.

Other paranormal activity witnessed at the Last Resort Bar include the vacuum cleaner turning on when it is not plugged in, sounds of running or movement inside the bar when no one is in there and creepy EVPs.

The bar owner has created a unique environment, featuring a collection of many of Aileen's belongings, including court documents, transcripts, copies of her letters and the bra she wore on her final night as a free woman. He also scattered a teaspoon of her ashes near a tree behind the bar.

The bar's mural includes Wuornos's last words: "I would like to say I'm sailing with the rock, and I'll be back, like Independence Day, with Jesus. June 6, like the movie. Big mothership and all, I'll be back, I'll be back."

It is evident that Aileen has returned to the Last Resort Bar, and many employees, patrons and paranormal researchers believe this is where she plans to spend her time in the afterlife.

Desert Inn Bar and Restaurant

Yeehaw Junction

Yeehaw Junction is a popular destination for those traveling across Florida from the west coast to the east coast and back again. It is also a popular place to stop when traveling along Florida's Turnpike, where weary travelers can fuel up, get food, use the restroom and take a break from a long day of driving. This area is surrounded by pastures and gas stations designed to give travelers everything they need before returning to the road.

Nestled on the quiet corner of State Route 60 and Kenansville Road, the Desert Inn now stands abandoned and in complete ruin. However, this dilapidated structure was the heart of the community in the 1880s, when it was used as a barroom and brothel for lumber runners and cowboys. The lounge area was where locals gathered for beverages and food, while upstairs housed a historic brothel suite, which was often used as a storage room many years after prostitution activity ceased in Yeehaw Junction.

The intersection where the Desert Inn is located first earned the name "Jackass Crossing" as a nod to the cowboys who used to tie up their mules used for work at the inn while they enjoyed a meal, a beer or a romp in the hay with one of the resident prostitutes. As travel through the area increased, it was renamed Yeehaw Junction because the original was highly offensive to weary travelers.

The Desert Inn did not have full-service electricity or water until 1978. The structure was added to the U.S. National Register of Historic Places in 1994, long before a semitruck hauling orange juice struck it.

Entering Yeehaw Junction via State Road 60 before approaching the haunted Desert Inn. *Heather Leigh, PhD.*

Businesses found along State Road 60 in Yeehaw Junction. *Aidan Carroll-Landon.*

Desert Inn Bar and Restaurant after it was struck twice by tractor trailers. *Aidan Carroll-Landon.*

For many years, owners of the Desert Inn hoped to turn the brothel suite into a museum and boost the local economy by rejuvenating the menu and lounge offerings to travelers needing a break. While waiting to be updated, the Desert Inn offered travelers opportunities to stay in one of the modern-day, yet still outdated, motel rooms behind the bar's main building.

The Desert Inn closed in June 2018, which is believed to be good because of the events that would happen the following year. On December 22, 2019, at 3:15 a.m., a semitruck hauling orange juice slammed into the restaurant, destroying more than one hundred years of history and memories. Since the bar and lounge were closed, no one was in the building when it was struck, eliminating any possible casualties caused by the crash.

Several employees and patrons of the Desert Inn have reported paranormal encounters and experiences. Many reported hearing bells jingling, seeing shadow figures and experiencing feelings of someone watching over their shoulders. Several people have reported witnessing items moving independently, including a chain lock on hotel room doors swinging back and forth.

Desert Inn Bar and Restaurant after it was struck twice by tractor trailers. *Aidan Carroll-Landon.*

When in the brothel suite, visitors witnessed a spirit appear in the mirror, believed to be a prostitute who once worked in the bar. Though the images were not found, some reports share information about this apparition being captured in the mirror in a photograph.

It is sad to know that the paranormal activity in the bar may continue but will never be experienced because the structure is in complete ruins and is expected to be demolished soon. But those who had the opportunity to come face to face with paranormal activity at the Desert Inn will never forget their experiences and hopefully will help the legend live on by sharing their stories.

GHOSTS OF A RINGLING BROTHER

SARASOTA

Part of the famous Ringling Brothers group, John Ringling and his wife, Mable, were longtime residents of Sarasota, Florida. At the height of the Ringling Brothers Circus endeavors, John wanted to build a life with his wife in the Sunshine State building Cà d'Zan (House of John), a waterfront mansion that is now the Ringling Museum.

John and his five brothers started the Ringling Brothers Circus in 1884, and John was in charge of overseeing the circus's show route. In this role, John persuaded his brothers in 1890 to expand the show's route to include destinations across the country, changing the show's method of transportation from wagons to railcars. At this time in the show's history, nearly one hundred railcars were used to transport the show across the United States each season.

In the 1920s, John and many others joined the Florida land boom, where he purchased and developed land in Sarasota. He also built the John Ringling Museum of Art with his wife to display the vast amounts of artwork he had collected while building his mansion and continuing to travel with the show. His art museum is now under the control and operation of Florida State University.

Mable died on June 8, 1929, of pneumonia at forty-four, and John died on December 2, 1936, at the age of seventy.

Though the couple died many moons ago, John, his wife and many other spirits are believed to haunt Cà d'Zan. People visiting claim to feel cold spots or a friendly presence while touring Cà d'Zan, while others have reported

Henry Ringling North, president and owner of the Ringling Brothers Circus, at the White House. *Harris & Ewing, Library of Congress.*

seeing a shadowy figure of a woman caught in the rose garden. Then, when approached, she suddenly disappears. John's apparition is seen on one of the home's many balconies as if he is overlooking his property.

The Ringling Brothers Circus Museum houses the largest miniature circus and is where many visitors see a spirit believed to be the circus priest who worked for the brothers in the 1920s.

The Keating Center at Ringling School of Art and Design was in the former Bay Haven Hotel, constructed in 1925. According to local legend, a prostitute named Mary, age eighteen or nineteen, who practiced her trade at the hotel was believed to have committed suicide by hanging herself. Some believe she was raped and murdered and did not commit suicide.

John purchased the hotel in 1931 after establishing his art school there. Many students and faculty living on the upper floors shared stories and reports of seeing Mary's apparition in the hallway and their rooms. Today, the building is part of the Ringling College of Art and Design, where some have seen Mary run across their room in a black nightgown and others claim to have been woken up by a bright glow in their room and the sounds of a shattering vase. Others have reported hearing terrifying scratching noises and, when opening their eyes, are met with a pale face staring back at them just inches away. When people say, "Go to bed, Mary," the activity stops. Other supernatural reports claim to experience furniture knocking over, paper scattered, unexplained footsteps and door knocks.

With the many paranormal experiences and encounters with John, Mable and Mary, it is safe to say the Ringling Museum and other structures in Sarasota are haunted by members of the Ringling Brothers Circus and those who used to call this area of town home.

Oldest Wooden Schoolhouse

St. Augustine

N ear the old city gate, nestled in the historic district of downtown St. Augustine, is the oldest wooden schoolhouse in America. This one-room classroom made it through centuries of war, disease and up-and-coming development and has become a piece of American education history.

The old schoolhouse is easily accessible and is like taking a step back to a simpler time, while hiding many community secrets, along with many spirits. Though the construction date for the schoolhouse is still being determined, it is believed it was built in the early eighteenth century, sometime between 1702 and 1716. It is set a few feet from Huguenot Cemetery, where countless victims died during the 1821 yellow fever epidemic and are buried. Many spirits remaining from the epidemic are believed to have made their way to this small, historic schoolhouse.

Since the mid-1930s, this one-room schoolhouse has been a small museum attraction for many travelers wanting to peek into St. Augustine's historic past. The museum features displays showcasing colonial life, artifacts, textbooks and a never-completed Grove of Educators. The Grove of Educators was an ambitious project to gather and showcase statues and artifacts of education pioneers from every country in the Americas. Sadly, only a few countries participated, and the collection remains incomplete.

Anyone who has visited St. Augustine knows there is no shortage of hauntings in the town, especially throughout the downtown historic district. The oldest wooden schoolhouse is no exception and is one of the paranormal hotspots in town.

The upstairs room, where the teacher lived with his family, is one of the most paranormally active locations of the old wooden schoolhouse. This area has gone untouched for many years, allowing the spirits to live in peace because the stairs are too old and fragile, making it unsafe for tourists and paranormal investigators to explore. However, there are many reports of hearing noises coming from upstairs. Some visitors don't know how to explain how they feel, but several have reported that moments after looking up the stairs, they are suddenly overwhelmed with a feeling that something is wrong.

Local legend claims the space underneath the stairs was once used as a child-sized dungeon where young children were locked in. During their imprisonment, these students were forced to think about their misdeeds before being allowed to emerge and return to their lessons with the rest of their schoolmates.

Many passersby have reported seeing a lone female figure standing in the second-story window. This woman is wearing white, and her hair is neatly pulled into a tight bun. She stands motionless while glaring over St. George Street as if waiting for someone to return. No one knows who this spirit is, but many believe she is the wife of the original schoolteacher, Juan Genoply. Others feel she is the mother of a former student who passed because of the effects of being locked for too long in the makeshift stairwell dungeon. The mother's spirit is trapped in the old schoolhouse forever as she seeks answers to what happened to her child. A third theory behind who or what is haunting the old schoolhouse in St. Augustine is the woman is a wandering spirit trying to find a place in the community to call home.

SULPHUR SPRINGS WATER TOWER

TAMPA

T ravel back in time to the late 1800s, when the Tampa area was home to serene mineral springs, igniting one developer's hopes and dreams. During the 1920s, Josiah Richardson wanted to make Sulphur Springs a tourist attraction themed around the healing waters that run through the area.

His first task was to build the Sulphur Springs Hotel and Apartment complex with Mave's Arcade, an indoor shopping venue on the hotel's ground floor. To meet the growing needs of the resort area and lack of water pressure, Richardson, with the assistance of Grover Poole, constructed a water tower overlooking the area. Richardson had to mortgage the resort to fund his new 200,000-gallon water tower.

The Sulphur Springs Water Tower was erected where a lighthouse once stood, helping light up the waters that flowed through the Tampa Bay area. The lighthouse had been used as a watchtower, keeping an eye out for dangerous pirates while aiding ship captains, lighting the way as they navigated Florida's Gulf coastline. The lighthouse was long gone, creating a dark spot on Tampa Bay's coastline before constructing the water tower. Today, the Sulphur Springs Water Tower is a historical landmark and can be seen from all around the area.

Plans to expand Richardson's tourist attraction included a luxurious spa and alligator farm to offer tours for visitors, but these two additions never became a reality. In 1933, the Tampa Electric Company dam was intentionally destroyed, causing water to swiftly rush toward Mave's Arcade

Sulphur Springs Hotel, 8122 North Nebraska Avenue, Tampa. *Library of Congress.*

and the hotel, damaging the structure and forcing shops to shutter. With the stores shutting down and the hotel's structure suffering extensive damage, Richardson's dreams were destroyed as he became bankrupt.

Then, the Great Depression swept across the country, leaving Sulphur Springs a desolate ghost town. In September 1929, when stock prices tanked, many people who felt there was no escape from the pain and depression associated with losing jobs and financial security turned to the tower, where they spent their final moments before leaping from it.

Later, a new drive-in theater was built under the shadows of the Sulphur Springs Water Tower, bringing new life to the area. The theater was the latest hangout, as many people would gather under a neon tower built to mimic the original water tower to watch one of the more than forty movies shown annually.

In 1985, the theater closed and left local officials debating for years about what would become of the now-vacant land. Eventually, this area became a park where locals enjoyed picnics, took walks and relaxed. However, gradually, the water tower fell victim to vandals, graffiti artists and time, leaving the structure less desirable and forcing many locals to look elsewhere for an outdoor space to enjoy.

In 1989, a massive restoration and painting project began with the help of Sherwin-Williams, which donated more than 150 gallons of graffiti-proof white paint. The new coat of paint gave the historic Sulphur Springs landmark new life.

The area around Sulphur Springs suffered much tragedy throughout the years, which could be the link between the living and the supernatural. Many visitors and explorers have experienced, witnessed and felt eerie, unexplainable happenings, forcing many to never return to the park underneath the historic water tower.

One paranormal legend from Sulphur Springs is that of the pirate ghosts and their ship that continued to search the shores of Tampa Bay and areas of Sulphur Springs. Many believe this paranormal activity is linked to the spot where the lighthouse they relied upon once stood. Since the lighthouse served as a marker for an infamous treasure map, today, the pirates continue to search the shores in the afterlife, hoping to unlock the secret to where the treasure was buried. Many locals, visitors and paranormal researchers have reported seeing pirates wandering the area looking lost and as if searching for something. There have also been many claims of seeing a transparent pirate ship sailing the waters near where the lighthouse once stood and disappearing as it approaches the shoreline.

Several paranormal stories around the Sulphur Springs Water Tower are related to the many deaths during the Depression. One commonly reported experience is seeing a man dressed in Depression-era clothing pacing back and forth at the top of the water tower. Several claim he has a gloomy appearance, almost as if he is contemplating his fate. After several minutes of wandering along the water tower's ledge, the man slowly fades away.

Sightings of a spectral woman have also been reported but have more of a devastating end than that of the man's appearance. This woman is often spotted at the top of the water tower, peering over the ledge with a tortured look. As she climbs over the railing, she leaps over the edge, jumping from the top of the tower. Passersby who have witnessed this event run to the woman's aid, but she disappears moments before impact. No one knows who the woman is or why she is meant to spend eternity reliving this horrific event. Still, it is a legend that draws many paranormal investigators to the park to capture a glimpse of the woman or the man who is spending the afterlife at the Sulphur Springs Tower.

THE CUBAN CLUB

YBOR CITY

Built in 1917, the Cuban Club, initially called Circulo Cubano, meaning circle of Cubans, is one of Ybor City's oldest and most haunted structures. This building in the Tampa area has the most historic background, mainly because it was once the gathering place for light-skinned Cuban immigrants in the early twentieth century.

Founded by Vincente Martinez-Ybor, Ybor City started as a parcel of land purchased from Tampa on which to build a cigar factory and provide housing for its workers. The cigar factory produced more than 500 million hand-rolled cigars in 1929 before the town suffered the effects of the Great Depression.

To attract workers, a small neighborhood with houses was built to provide a place for employees to live with their families near where they worked. Throughout the years, the community of cigar factory workers grew, and it is now known as one of Tampa's most breathtaking neighborhoods with awe-inspiring architecture.

Today's Cuban Club structure was built in the exact location to replace the original structure, which burned down. As it was no longer serving as a cigar factory, the structure was modified and updated to serve the community as a place to gather for educational classes, business meetings, social gatherings and parties. The building is home to a spacious ballroom and a theater and was once home to a bowling alley, restaurant, spa, swimming pool and conference-style rooms for social gatherings. At one point in the building's history, a medical clinic was onsite. Today, it serves the community as a multi-use rental facility.

In addition to being one of the most beautiful structures in the Tampa area, the Cuban Club is one of the most haunted locations in the United States. Whatever and whoever haunts this historic structure remains behind because of its eerie past. The paranormal activity at this location is believed to be linked to the theory that spirits tend to gravitate to where they were the happiest. Back then, social clubs allowed immigrants to laugh, socialize and enjoy time with others like them.

Owners, employees, visitors and paranormal researchers have concluded that at least three hundred spirits call the Cuban Club home. One of the most commonly encountered spirits is of an eight-year-old boy known as Little Jimmy, who is believed to have drowned in the basement, which was once home to Ybor City's only swimming pool. Reports claim his drowning was an accident, and no foul play was involved. Many who have come face to face with Little Jimmy report seeing him peeking out from behind curtains and peering out from the upstairs window, as has been captured in photographs.

Another spirit hanging around the Ybor City club is Victorio, who was a playwright believed to have taken his own life in 1919. Many believe his spirit haunts the club's theater after committing suicide when he forgot the words to his debut play. Several witnesses have seen his spirit wandering the theater's second floor, looking distraught and stressed.

The spirit of a woman named Rosalita is known to hang out in the third-floor ballroom, where it is rumored she was thrown off the balcony after rejecting a young man's request to dance. Many have seen her standing there looking over the dance floor, while others have reported her standing stationary, only slightly swaying back and forth, as if waiting for the perfect suitor to ask her to dance.

The apparition of a woman wearing a white dress is also spotted roaming the halls of the Cuban Club. It is uncertain if this woman is the spirit of Rosalita or another woman looking for something as she roams the halls of the infamous club.

Other paranormal claims experienced at the Cuban Club include hearing strange noises, disembodied voices and sounds of a piano playing soft, sorrowful tunes. Some have also reported seeing what can only be explained as ghost lights. Many have spotted strange, unexplainable lights on the stage that flicker as if there is an electrical issue, but the lights appear on the stage where no lights are installed. Some believe these lights are the spirit's way of communicating with the living.

Undoubtedly, the Cuban Club is haunted, making this location a number-one place for paranormal investigators to visit.

Everglades Lounge
at the Clewiston Inn

Clewiston

The historic Clewiston Inn is a popular destination for travelers looking for a historic place to stay that holds the many secrets of Florida's past. Nestled in the Clewiston Inn is the Everglades Lounge, popular among locals and visitors, housing a unique wraparound mural of the Florida Everglades. Plus, this bar is the perfect place to hang out and make new friends while waiting to glimpse the inn's friendly female ghost.

For over eighty years, people have enjoyed staying in the rooms at the Clewiston Inn and enjoying the company they are surrounded with, including the supernatural entities they often encounter during a visit.

As the "Sweetest Town in America,"[12] Clewiston, Florida, is set on the southwest side of Lake Okeechobee and is known for producing sugar cane, citrus and many vegetables and raising cattle. The small town has a population under 7,500, and many residents would like to increase the number of residents by a few because they consider the ghostly residents part of the community.

Several of these spirits enjoy spending time at the Clewiston Inn, where it is believed four different spirits are lingering within the walls of the famous inn. One spirit, believed to be Anita Conklin, who lived at the Clewiston Inn, is often felt in room 225. Conklin died in 1994, and many visitors claim to have had their hair pulled by her when in the room and believe it is her message and way of attempting to keep people out of the room.

Paranormal experiences also occur in room 118 of the Clewiston Inn, where many people have spotted the apparition of a woman looking out the window when no one is in the room.

Staff at the inn have reported walking into the kitchen late at night to the sounds of clanging pots and pans. Several employees claim they are scared to be in the kitchen alone late at night.

As a historical landmark in Clewiston, the inn has been renovated many times. Still, the owners do everything possible to maintain its historical presence by keeping much of the original furniture and wood paneling. Because of the efforts to preserve historical value, the inn continues to attract spirits wanting to return to a place they once loved and paranormal enthusiasts who love history and want to come face to face with one of the inn's famous ghostly residents.

Luckily, the ghosts and spirits peacefully reside together at the Clewiston Inn, and many people claim this location is a very spiritual place. With more people becoming open about their paranormal experiences, others are learning about hidden haunted gems like the Clewiston Inn.

NOTES

1. "Florida Attraction—Ripley's Believe It or Not!" 2023, www.ripleys. com/florida.
2. "Spook Hill—Things to Do Lake Wales," Visit Central Florida, visitcentralflorida.org/featured/spook-hill.
3. Spook Hill Elementary, "About Our School," spookhill.polkschoolsfl. com/school_info/about_our_school.
4. Sunken Gardens Forever Foundation, "About the Gardens," sunkengardensfoundation.org/about-the-gardens.
5. City of Orlando, "Greenwood Cemetery," www.orlando.gov/Our-Government/Departments-Offices/Executive-Offices/City-Clerk/Greenwood-Cemetery.
6. Norris McWhirter, *1981 Guinness Book of World Records* (n.p., 1981).
7. Kevin M. McCarthy, *The Hippocrene U.S.A. Guide to Black Florida* (New York: Hippocrene Books, 1995).
8. Craig Myers, "Gulf Breeze UFO Model Found," *Pensacola News Journal*, June 10, 1990, 1A, archived April 3, 2022, at the Wayback Machine.
9. Abandoned Florida, "New Smyrna Old Sugar Mill Ruins," November 15, 2015, www.abandonedfl.com/new-smyrna-old-sugar-mill-ruins.
10. Florida Back Roads Travel, "The Ancient Spanish Monastery," www. florida-backroads-travel.com/the-ancient-spanish-monastery.html.
11. "Ghostly Lights Still a Mystery; Oviedo Apparition Never Been Explained," *Orlando Sentinel*, August 5, 1990, www.orlandosentinel. com/1990/08/05/ghostly-lights-still-a-mystery-oviedo-apparition-never-been-explained.
12. WFLX.com, "Spirits Felt at Historic Florida Inn," January 5, 2009, www.wflx.com/story/9616647/spirits-felt-at-historic-florida-inn.

BIBLIOGRAPHY

"Barefoot Mailman | Hillsboro." Lighthouse Scenic Tours. www.
    lighthousescenictours.com/barefoot-mailman.
"Bok Tower Gardens, Florida Attraction | Lake Wales." n.d. Visit Central
    Florida. visitcentralflorida.org/featured/bok-tower-gardens.
"Braden Castle Ruins." Atlas Obscura. www.atlasobscura.com/places/
    braden-castle-ruins.
"The Brownie Story." Brownie the Town Dog of Daytona Beach,
    November 15, 2017. www.browniethetowndog.org/the-brownie-story.
Buehn, Debra W. "Old Clay County Jail Stars in Local Haunts' TV
    Show Sunday." *Florida Times-Union*. www.jacksonville.com/story/news/
    local/2010/04/02/old-clay-county-jail-stars-local-haunts-tv-show-
    sunday/15950770007
Burke, Michael. "'Jim': UFO Pictures Not Fake." *Pensacola News Journal*,
    October 23, 1988, 29A.
"Coral Castle Museum." 2018. coralcastle.com.
"The Cuban Club Is One of the Oldest Ybor Buildings—and One of
    the Most Haunted in the U.S." FOX 13 News, October 29, 2021.
    www.fox13news.com/news/the-cuban-club-is-one-of-the-oldest-ybor-
    building-and-one-of-the-most-haunted-in-the-u-s.
"Dames Point Bridge." Haunted Places, October 8, 2015. www.
    hauntedplaces.org/item/dames-point-bridge.
Díaz, Ma del Rosario Castro. "This Church in North Miami Beach Is One
    of the Oldest Buildings in the Western Hemisphere." Secret Miami,
    December 9, 2021. secretmiami.com/ancient-spanish-monastery-miami.

"Dr. Samuel A. Mudd House Museum." drmudd.org.

"Dr. Samuel Mudd and the Civil War." Dry Tortugas. www.drytortugas. com/samuel-mudd-civil-war.

"Dry Tortugas Dispatch: Beckoning Birds, a Lighthouse, and No Ghost." WLRN, February 20, 2013. www.wlrn.org/culture/2013-02-20/dry-tortugas-dispatch-beckoning-birds-a-lighthouse-and-no-ghost.

"Edward Ball Wakulla Springs State Park." Florida State Parks. www. floridastateparks.org/WakullaSprings.

Fillmore Correspondent, Andy. "Ghosts in the Barker House?" *Star Banner*. www.ocala.com/news/20190224/ocala-paranormal-group-investigates-ma-barker-house.

"Florida Lighthouses—Ponce de Leon Lighthouse." www.ponceinlet.org.

"Florida's Only Presidential Museum." Truman Little White House. www. trumanlittlewhitehouse.org.

"Fountain of Youth." St. Augustine & Ponte Vedra, FL. www. floridashistoriccoast.com/things-to-do/history/fountain-youth.

"Ghostly Warning: Dead Gangster Ma Barker Doesn't Want Her House Moved." *Tampa Bay Times*. www.tampabay.com/features/humaninterest/ghostly-warning-dead-gangster-ma-barker-doesnt-want-her-house-moved/2300286.

"The Ghosts of the St. Augustine Lighthouse | Haunted Lighthouse." Ghost City Tours. ghostcitytours.com/st-augustine/haunted-places/st-augustine-lighthouse.

"The Ghost Town Left behind by an American Sect of Hollow Earth Believers." Messy Nessy Chic, August 31, 2021. www.messynessychic. com/2021/08/31/the-ghost-town-left-behind-by-an-american-sect-of-hollow-earth-believers.

"Ghostwatching? Here's Where to Go." *Jax Daily Record*, December 13, 2001. www.jaxdailyrecord.com/news/2001/dec/13/ghostwatching-heres-where-go.

Gibson, Andrew. "Infamous Florida: Serial Killer Aileen Wuornos Drank Here." *Orlando Sentinel*, May 12, 2015. www.orlandosentinel. com/2015/05/12/infamous-florida-serial-killer-aileen-wuornos-drank-here.

"Haunted Chokoloskee: The Wraith of Smallwood Trading Post." Backpackerverse, July 23, 2016. backpackerverse.com/haunted-chokoloskee-the-wraith-of-smallwood-trading-post.

"Haunted Coral Castle." Miami Haunts, December 27, 2019. miamihaunts.com/9-haunted-coral-castle.

"The Haunted History of Captain Tony's Saloon in Key West." Ghosts & Gravestones. www.ghostsandgravestones.com/key-west/captain-tonys-saloon.

"Historic Key West Cemetery Is Full of Fascinating Stories." Florida Rambler, August 1, 2023. www.floridarambler.com/historic-florida-getaways/key-west-cemetery.

"Historic Lake Wales." historiclakewales.com/spookhill.

"History of Devil's Millhopper." Florida State Parks. www.floridastateparks.org/learn/history-devils-millhopper.

"Home." Bok Tower Gardens. boktowergardens.org.

"HOME." Skunkape. www.skunkape.info.

"Homegrown Haunts: Orlando Ghost Stories." Orange County Regional History Center, October 19, 2020. www.thehistorycenter.org/homegrown-haunts.

James, Eddie. "A Few Ghost Stories: Brownie Died on Halloween." Brownie the Town Dog of Daytona Beach, October 18, 2017. www.browniethetowndog.org/a-few-ghost-stories-brownie-died-on-halloween.

"Johnnie Brown and Laddie Best of Friends." Ghosts of Palm Beach. ghostsofpalmbeach.com/blog/johnnie-brown-and-laddie-best-of-friend.

"John's Pass Bridge." Florida Haunted Houses. www.floridahauntedhouses.com/real-haunt/johns-pass-bridge.html.

Jones, Colleen Michele. "10 Things You Probably Didn't Know about Ripley's Believe It or Not! in St. Augustine." *St. Augustine Record*. www.staugustine.com/story/entertainment/2021/10/06/ripleys-believe-not-st-augustine-full-surprises/6018233001.

Jones, Robert R. *Florida Ghost Stories*. Lanham, MD: Rowman & Littlefield, 2013.

"Key West Haunted Cemeteries." Ghosts & Gravestones. www.ghostsandgravestones.com/key-west/cemeteries.

"Koreshan Ghosts Tell the Tale of Their Utopian Community." WGCU PBS & NPR for Southwest Florida, January 31, 2018. news.wgcu.org/news/2018-01-31/koreshan-ghosts-tell-the-tale-of-their-utopian-community.

"The Legend of Juan Ponce de León." Ghost City Tours. ghostcitytours.com/st-augustine/ghost-stories/ponce-de-leon.

"The Macabre History of Florida's Oldest Bar." Atlas Obscura. www.atlasobscura.com/places/captain-tony-s-saloon.

Marino, Sara. "Part of Historic Desert Inn Near Orlando Collapses after Semitrailer Hits Building." Treasure Coast Newspapers, December 22, 2019.

Nelander, John. "From the Archives: Coral Cut of Horrors? Spooky Legends Spring Up at Palm Beach Coral Cut." *Palm Beach Daily News*. www.palmbeachdailynews.com/story/entertainment/ holiday/2018/10/31/from-archives-coral-cut-of-horrors-spooky-legends-spring-up-at-palm-beach-coral-cut/9405518007.

"Old Town Manor Legends of Captain Tony's Saloon." Old Town Manor. oldtownmanor.com/captaintonys.

"Ponce de Leon Inlet Lighthouse." Daytona Beach. www.daytonabeach. com/things-to-do/attractions/ponce-inlet-lighthouse.

Richardson, Dave. "Expert Still Calls UFO Hoax." *Pensacola News Journal*, April 22, 1988, 1A.

"Ripley's Believe It or Not! Museum." St. Augustine & Ponte Vedra, FL. www. floridashistoriccoast.com/directory/ripleys-believe-it-or-not-museum.

"ROBERT the DOLL." robertthedoll.org.

Roseboom, Matt. "Is Titanic—The Experience Actually Haunted? Ghost Tours Offer a Chance to Hear Staff Tales." *Attractions Magazine*, October 15, 2013. attractionsmagazine.com/is-titanic-the-experience-actually-haunted-ghost-tours-offer-a-chance-to-hear-staff-tales.

Shurba, Nicolette. "Explore the Historical and Haunted Side of Orlando." *Orlando Weekly*. www.orlandoweekly.com/orlando/explore-the-historical-and-haunted-side-of-orlando/Content?oid=16978460.

"Skunk Ape Research Headquarters, Ochopee, Florida." Roadside America. www.roadsideamerica.com/story/13341.

"Spooky Places in the Bradenton Area." Bradenton Gulf Islands. www. bradentongulfislands.com/pages/267/spooky-places-in-the-bradenton-area.

"St. Augustine Historical Attraction." Fountain of Youth, 2018. www. fountainofyouthflorida.com.

"St. Augustine Museums | St. Augustine Attractions." Potters Wax Museum. www.potterswaxmuseum.com.

"Strange Graves: The Bound Woman of Key West Cemetery." Cult of Weird, April 11, 2016. www.cultofweird.com/death/bound-woman-key-west-cemetery.

"Sugar Mill Ruins." Volusia, February 25, 2016. www.volusia.org/services/ community-services/parks-recreation-and-culture/parks-and-trails/ park-facilities-and-locations/historical-parks/sugar-mill-ruins.stml.

"Sunken Gardens." St. Pete. www.stpete.org/visitors/sunken_gardens.php.

"10 Scary Urban Legends, Haunted Places to Visit in Central Florida." FOX 35 Orlando, October 11, 2022. www.fox35orlando.com/news/10-central-florida-urban-legends-haunted-places-just-in-time-for-spooky-season.

"Titanic the Experience Discovers Paranormal Activity?" Mynews13. www.mynews13.com/fl/orlando/news/2012/9/10/titanic_the_experien.

"Tractor Trailer Crashes into Desert Inn and Restaurant in Yeehaw Junction." WPTV, December 22, 2019.

"UFO Sightings Puts Gulf Breeze on Extraterrestrial Map." *Orlando Sentinel*, January 22, 2008. www.orlandosentinel.com/2008/01/22/ufo-sightings-puts-gulf-breeze-on-extraterrestrial-map.

"ValuJet Flight 592 Crash Site: 'Walking Dead' Seen in the Everglades." *Journal News*, August 26, 2021. journalnews.com.ph/valujet-flight-592-crash-site-walking-dead-seen-in-the-everglades/.

Warren, Michael. "Florida's Old Brick Road—The Dixie Highway." Floridatraveler.com, April 30, 2017. floridatraveler.com/florida-ghost-highway.

West, Cindy. "UFO Fever Strikes West Florida." *Pensacola News Journal*, March 5, 1989, 130.

"Why Do Cars Roll Uphill at Spook Hill? Legends & Science Explain the Thrill of Lake Wales' Gravity Hill." FOX 13 News, October 31, 2022. www.fox13news.com/news/why-do-cars-roll-uphill-at-spook-hill-legends-science-explains-the-thrill-of-lake-wales-gravity-hill.

"World Famous Glass Bottom Boats." Silver Springs State Park. silversprings.com.

"You Can Have a Terrifying Alien Encounter at This WEIRD Waterfall in Gainesville." Backpackerverse, March 11, 2017. backpackerverse.com/waterfall-millhopper-gainesville.

Zizo, Christie. "Find a Ghostly Encounter at These 15 Haunted Places in Central Florida." WKMG, October 10, 2022. www.clickorlando.com/news/local/2022/10/10/find-a-ghostly-encounter-at-these-15-haunted-places-in-central-florida.

ABOUT THE AUTHOR

Heather Leigh Carroll-Landon, PhD, started her journey in the paranormal field as a teenager after multiple interactions with her grandfather, who passed away many years before. She has researched and traveled to locations to learn more about the history of the land, buildings and local area and paranormal claims. As long as she has been interested in the supernatural, Heather Leigh has been a freelance writer, writing for several newspapers, magazines and online publications. She and her family (Exploration Paranormal) appeared in *Real Haunts: Ghost Towns and Real Haunts 3*, where they explored many southern Nevada ghost towns, and she has appeared on *Ghost Adventures: Lake of Death*.

She is an author of articles and books and a lecturer about all things paranormal. Her first book, *Haunted Southern Nevada Ghost Towns*, was published by The History Press in August 2022, and her second book, *Ghosts and Legends of the Vegas Valley*, was also published by The History Press in February 2023. These books were followed by her most recent books, *Haunted Florida Lighthouses*, which was published in September 2023, and *Haunted Florida Ghost Towns*, which was published in March 2024. She has many more book ideas in the works and hopes to bring them to life in the near future.

She holds a doctor of philosophy degree in metaphysical and humanistic science with a specialty in paranormal science. She is a certified paranormal investigator and a certified EVP technician. She aims to help others take a more scientific approach to paranormal investigations and research.

Heather Leigh is also the founder of Exploration Paranormal. She hosts *Exploring the Paranormal* and co-hosts *Ghost Education 101* with Philip R. Wyatt and *Passport to the Paranormal* with Joe Franke, also on Facebook and YouTube. You can find Heather Leigh on Facebook (@DrHeatherLeigh), where you will find additional information, including upcoming classes, lectures and more, or via her websites, www.heatherleighphd.com and www. explorationparanormal.com.